Life During the Spanish Inquisition

Other titles in the *Living History* series include:

Life During the Spanish Inquisition

Adam Woog

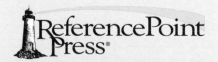

ReferencePoint
Press®

San Diego, CA

© 2015 ReferencePoint Press, Inc.
Printed in the United States

For more information, contact:
ReferencePoint Press, Inc.
PO Box 27779
San Diego, CA 92198
www.ReferencePointPress.com

LIBRARY OF CONGRESS CATALOGING-IN-PUBLICATION DATA

Woog, Adam, 1953-
    Life during the Spanish Inquisition / by Adam Woog.
        pages cm. -- (Living history)
    Includes bibliographical references and index.
    ISBN 978-1-60152-722-6 (hardback) -- ISBN 1-60152-722-5 (hardback) 1. Inquisition--Spain--
Juvenile literature. 2. Spain--Church history--Juvenile literature. I. Title.
    BX1735.W66   2015
    272'.2--dc23

                                                            2014013327

Contents

Foreword

History is a complex and multifaceted discipline that embraces many different areas of human activity. Given the expansive possibilities for the study of history, it is significant that since the advent of formal writing in the Ancient Near East over six thousand years ago, the contents of most nonfiction historical literature have been overwhelmingly limited to politics, religion, warfare, and diplomacy.

Beginning in the 1960s, however, the focus of many historical works experienced a substantive change worldwide. This change resulted from the efforts and influence of an ever-increasing number of progressive contemporary historians who were entering the halls of academia. This new breed of academician, soon accompanied by many popular writers, argued for a major revision of the study of history, one in which the past would be presented from the ground up. What this meant was that the needs, wants, and thinking of ordinary people should and would become an integral part of the human record. As British historian Mary Fulbrook wrote in her 2005 book, *The People's State: East German Society from Hitler to Honecker,* students should be able to view "history with the people put back in." This approach to understanding the lives and times of people of the past has come to be known as social history. According to contemporary social historians, national and international affairs should be viewed not only from the perspective of those empowered to create policy but also through the eyes of those over whom power is exercised.

The American historian and best-selling author, Louis "Studs" Terkel, was one of the pioneers in the field of social history. He is best remembered for his oral histories, which were firsthand accounts of everyday life drawn from the recollections of interviewees who lived during pivotal events or periods in history. Terkel's first book, *Division Street America* (published in 1967), focuses on urban living in and around Chicago and is a compilation of seventy interviews of immigrants and native-born Americans. It was followed by several other oral histories including *Hard Times* (the 1930s depression), *Working* (people's feelings about their jobs), and his 1985 Pulitzer Prize–winning *The Good War* (about life in America before, during, and after World War II).

In keeping with contemporary efforts to present history by people and about people, ReferencePoint's *Living History* series offers students a journey through recorded history as recounted by those who lived it. While modern sources such as those found in *The Good War* and on radio and TV interviews are readily available, those dating to earlier periods in history are scarcer and often more obscure the further back in time one investigates. These important primary sources are there nonetheless waiting to be discovered in literary formats such as posters, letters, and diaries, and in artifacts such as vases, coins, and tombstones. And they are also found in places as varied as ancient Mesopotamia, Charles Dickens's England, and Nazi concentration camps. The *Living History* series uncovers these and other available sources as they relate the "living history" of real people to their student readers.

1480
The first Spanish Inquisition tribunal becomes active in Seville.

1391
In the first major uprising against Spanish Jews, at least one hundred thousand are massacred and hundreds of thousands forcibly baptized.

1479
Ferdinand becomes king of his domain of Aragon, furthering the royal couple's plan to unify Spain—which included the forced conversion of non-Catholics.

1469
Prince Ferdinand of Aragon and Princess Isabella of Castile marry, merging their respective kingdoms to lay the foundation for a united Spain.

1400 ••• 1460　　1465　　1470　　1475　　1480

1474
Isabella becomes queen of her domain of Castile.

1458
The first edition of Bishop Alphonso de Spina's influential document *Fortalitium Fidei* is published.

1478
Pope Sixtus IV authorizes the Spanish Inquisition at the request of Ferdinand and Isabella.

1481
The first inquisitional trial is held, with six people condemned and burned alive in Seville.

the Spanish Inquisition

1483
Tomás de Torquemada becomes chief inquisitor for several regions of Spain.

1488
Torquemada is named first inquisitor-general of the Spanish Inquisition.

1502
All Muslims are ordered to be converted or expelled from Spain.

1826
The last person to be condemned by the Inquisition, schoolteacher Cayetano Ripoll, is executed.

1480   1485   1490   1495   1500 ••• 1600 ••• 1800

1485
A priest and prominent figure in the Inquisition, Pedro de Arbués, is assassinated.

1614
Islam is officially banned in Spain.

1492
The Alhambra Edict orders all Jews expelled from Spain.

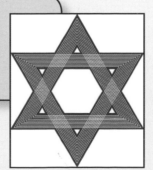

1834
The Spanish Inquisition officially ends.

The Grip of the Spanish Inquisition

Riding donkeys or mules, a group of people is paraded through the narrow cobblestone streets of a medieval town to the main plaza. They are weak from months of imprisonment, mistreatment, and malnutrition. They are clothed in rough, uncomfortable garments. Black-robed monks walk alongside, praying and chanting aloud. Behind them comes a long procession of officials and a town crier, who announces the crimes of the condemned as they march.

The procession halts at shrines and churches along the way, and by the time it arrives at the plaza a large crowd has gathered. A daylong session of religious rituals follows, including elaborate purification ceremonies and fervent sermons describing how the convicts have sinned against God. When the crowd is at a fever pitch, the climactic moment arrives: The prisoners are tied to stakes and burned alive.

> **WORDS IN CONTEXT**
> **heresy**
> Dissent or criticism of the Church's teachings and beliefs.

This was an auto-da-fé ("act of faith"), the most terrifying aspect of a terrifying era: Spain's long centuries of irrational hatred toward those whose religion and culture were different. At the center of this terror, which peaked in the late fourteenth and early fifteenth centuries, was the Spanish Inquisition—an institution whose name is still synonymous with cruelty, persecution, fear, and intolerance.

Religious conflict did not begin with the Spanish Inquisition, and it certainly did not end with it. It is all too common even today. But the stranglehold that the Inquisition had on Spain was one of the worst events in the history of religious hatred and persecution. So it remains a powerful symbol of how intolerance can destroy lives. Historian Toby Green comments, "This is, in the end, . . . a story whose relevance never vanishes, a warning from the past."[1]

The Inquisition's Targets

The Spanish Inquisition was an arm of the Catholic Church dedicated to finding and punishing suspected heretics—that is, anyone who questioned, defied, or simply did not belong to the church. It was a highly organized and ruthless bureaucracy overseen by an inquisitor-general, who had below him a vast system of regional courts and their employees. Together this army of terror collected information, threw suspects in jail, and put them on trial. Sometimes it used torture to force confessions. And if found guilty, the victim faced punishment ranging from a light reprimand or a fine to the worst penalty: death by burning.

The Inquisition's primary targets were Spain's Jewish population and, to a lesser extent, its smaller Muslim population. Distrust and hatred of the Jews, and preaching against them by Church authorities, had existed for centuries in Spain before the Inquisition was born. Prejudice then took some forms familiar even today: People believed that those who were not like them were dirty, untrustworthy, and inferior. The language used by Andrés Bernáldez, a priest and historian who lived during the era, reflects the virulent hatred held by some and their desire to wipe out anyone who did not believe as they did. Bernáldez noted that Friar Vincent Ferrer, a religious leader of the fourteenth century, "wanted to convert all the Jews of Spain [and destroy their] obstinate, stinking synagogue."[2]

Many Jews tried to retain their religious practice despite the threat they faced. They continued to trust that they would survive. An observer of the period wrote, "They lived with that hope that . . . God would miraculously sustain and defend them, and held that they would be

> **WORDS IN CONTEXT**
>
> *converso*
>
> A Jew or Muslim who converted to Christianity.

An auto-da-fé (act of faith) was a formal ceremony employed during the Spanish Inquisition where heretics would be sentenced for their crimes against the Catholic Church. Sometimes the church-sanctioned sentence, carried out by the civil authorities, would be public burning at the stake (pictured).

removed from the Christians through the hand of God, and taken to the Holy Promised Land. They . . . lived among Christians with these crazy beliefs, in such a way that the whole lineage remained defamed and touched by this sickness."[3]

The number of Jews to retain their religion was relatively small. The majority of them chose to convert to Catholicism. These converts were called *conversos*. (Historians also call them New Christians. The Catholic Church underwent a split in the 1500s; during this period and throughout the Inquisition, the terms Catholic and Christian both referred to the branch that is now called Catholicism.)

At first the Inquisition did not target all *conversos*. Instead, it focused on *conversos* who were accused of practicing their original religions in secrecy. To the Catholic Church this was considered a most terrible sin. Within decades of its formation, however, the Inquisition expanded its scope. Its targets now included all Jews and Muslims: *conversos*, false *conversos*, and those who still openly observed their own religions. The Inquisition also investigated Catholics suspected of helping anyone accused of heresy (dissent or criticism of the Church's teachings and beliefs). And it further targeted Catholics who had fallen away from the church or who dared to question it. The Inquisition wanted to "reconcile" these former Catholics—that is, bring them back to the church.

> **WORDS IN CONTEXT**
> **reconcile**
> To return to the church after falling away.

Exact figures for the number of victims of the Inquisition are not known, and estimates vary considerably. However, noted authority Henry Kamen estimates that roughly 130,000 people faced trials between 1540 and 1700. During that period, Kamen surmises, the Inquisition caused some two thousand deaths, including those who died in prison. The terrors of the Inquisition touched virtually everyone in Spain—and it changed forever the lives of many.

Chapter One

The Inquisition Comes to Spain

In the earliest centuries of the Catholic Church, beginning in the first century CE, clergy across Europe had periodically targeted suspected heretics (including anyone accused of witchcraft or sorcery). The same went for those accused of immoral acts such as adultery. Sometimes the punishment was relatively light—perhaps paying a fine or having to say certain prayers. But convicted heretics also faced brutal punishment or death.

Rooting Out Heretics and Witches

In 1252 the pope—the supreme leader of the church—issued an order that torture was allowed—but only to obtain a confession, not as a punishment. He stated that a religious leader could authorize torture as a way to achieve this goal, within certain bounds. The order stated that a priest "has the authority to oblige all heretics that he may have in his power, without breaking limbs or endangering their lives, to confess their errors."[4]

Suspected or convicted heretics did not face only the threat of physical punishment; penalties could also be mental or spiritual. For a Catholic the most horrifying punishment by far was excommunication—that is, expulsion from the church. This meant being barred from heaven after death and suffering an eternity in hell.

The most famous victim of an early inquisition was a young French-

WORDS IN CONTEXT

excommunication

The banishment of a person from Christianity, which bars that person from entering heaven.

woman, Joan of Arc, who in 1430–1431 stood trial for heresy. Claiming to be divinely directed, she had inspired French troops to battle against England. But she was brutally executed by pro-British clergy for the sin of claiming to hear the voice of God. Writer Kathryn Harrison notes, "For refusing to renounce the voices that guided her as deviltry, Joan, 19 years old, was burned at the stake before a jeering crowd, her charred body displayed to anyone who cared to examine it."[5]

In addition to targeting heretics such as Joan, early inquisitions also focused on rooting out alleged witches and sorcerers who practiced black magic and were blamed for a variety of disasters. Notable among these was a long period of freezing weather that began in the fourteenth century, destroying crops and killing millions of people across Europe. In 1484 the pope authorized inquisitions to punish those held responsible for this catastrophe. He stated:

> It has recently come to our ears [that] many persons of both sexes, heedless of their own salvation and forsaking the Catholic faith, give themselves over to devils male and female, and by their incantations, charms, and conjurings, and by other abominable superstitions and sortileges [sorceries], offences, crimes, and misdeeds, ruin and cause to perish the offspring of women, the foal of animals, the products of the earth, the grapes of vines, and the fruits of trees, as well as men and women, cattle and flocks and herds and animals of every kind, vineyards also and orchards, meadows, pastures, harvests, grains and other fruits of the earth.[6]

Similarities and Differences

Early inquisitions began in cities and towns across Europe, notably in France in the twelfth century CE. These early inquisitions laid the groundwork in several ways for the Spanish Inquisition. For example, people were obliged to report suspected heretics—even family and friends—to the church. In the thirteenth century the then-current pope stated that good Catholics had an obligation to accuse others whom they suspected to be "true assassins of souls and thieves of the Sacraments of

This nineteenth-century painting by French artist Frederic Legrip depicts Joan of Arc being burned at the stake as a heretic. Joan, the so-called Maid of Orleans and French national hero, is one of the earliest and most famous victims of the Christian Church's feared inquisitions.

God and of the Christian faith . . . just as robbers and thieves of temporal goods are obliged to accuse their accomplices and confess the evil that they have done."[7]

There were other practices that early inquisitions passed on to the Spanish Inquisition. For example, trials required a minimum of two witnesses, who testified that heretical acts had taken place. The trials also offered the accused a chance to freely confess any form of heresy, which freed them of punishment for their sins. Another practice that the Spanish Inquisition kept was the imprisonment of an accused person during his or her trial, which could last months or even years.

But there were also differences between early inquisitions and the Spanish version. Notably, the latter had a much more organized structure and oversight. For example, although the pope sanctioned early inquisitors, they operated independently, with no central authority dictating their methods or overseeing trials. The early tribunals thus could set their own rules to a large degree regarding factors such as the degree of punishment. Also, the early inquisitors required little or no evidence to justify a trial. Typically, only an accusation was enough to put someone in danger. On the other hand, the Spanish Inquisition had relatively strict rules about deciding who could be tried. Not everyone was as vulnerable as in previous times.

> **WORDS IN CONTEXT**
> **tribunal**
> A court of justice.

Convivencia

Although the threat of an inquisitional trial was always present, prior to the Spanish Inquisition, Muslims, Jews, and Catholics in Spain had coexisted for centuries in relative peace. This environment was called *convivencia*. In some ways, the three groups mingled relatively freely. For example, Jews often stood beside Catholics at the baptisms of their children, and Catholics did likewise at Jewish circumcision ceremonies. Also, intermarriage, especially between Jews and Catholics, was not uncommon. As a result, some historians estimate, by the end of the fifteenth century most of Spain's noble families had at least some Jewish ancestry.

They also connected in matters such as business deals or other forms of contracts. For example, Jews were noted for their medical skills, and Catholics often used the services of Jewish doctors. One instance of this came in 1406, when a Catholic man in the region of Aragon made a contract with a Jewish doctor to treat his son's head wound. The contract stated, "I, Miguel de Pertusa, make this contract with you Isaac Abenforma son of don Salomon and I promise that even if he dies I shall satisfy and pay you."[8]

In Their Own Words

Fierce Words

Priests and everyday people alike often used fiery language to express the hatred they felt against minorities, even those who had converted to Catholicism. In this passage, Alphonso de Spina, a monk who was one of the forces behind the formation of the Inquisition, summed up this belief when he wrote that a *converso* is

> no more than a filthy Jew in Christian disguise . . . the despised, damned and detested generation of baptized Jews and all those descended from their accursed lineage of adulterers sunk in disbelief and infidelity, fathers of all greed, sowers of all discord and division, abounding in malice and perverseness, eternal ingrates against God, violators of His commandments, deviators from His ways.

Quoted in John Edward Longhurst, "The Age of Torquemada," *Library of Iberian Resources Online.* http://libro.uca.edu.

To a lesser extent, Jews and Catholics also interacted with Muslims. For example, they sometimes invited Muslim friends to attend religious ceremonies and on occasion hired Muslim musicians to play for celebrations. On the whole, however, Muslims were generally less assimilated than Jews into everyday Spanish society. They tended to keep to themselves to a greater degree. According to historian Joseph Pérez, Muslims "lived on the margins of [Catholic] society rather than intermingling with it, as the Jews did."[9]

On the other hand, during the era of *convivencia* the three groups kept some aspects of their personal lives separate; for example, they typically lived in separate neighborhoods and kept their own customs and practices, such as those of language, music, and food. And while many historians consider *convivencia* to be a period of genuine coexistence, others assert that this did not include equality in social status. They argue that Catholics always held the upper hand and generally treated Jews and Muslims as second-class citizens. Henry Kamen notes, "Communities of Christians, Jews, and Muslims never lived together on equal terms; so-called convivencia was always a relationship between unequals. Within that inequality, the minorities played their roles while attempting to avoid conflicts."[10]

This inequality was one reason that the peace of *convivencia* was not universal. Prejudice against religious minorities occasionally sparked violence. For example, Andrés Bernáldez, the sixteenth-century priest and chronicler, wrote about a riot and its aftermath that occurred in the early fifteenth century, following an unsuccessful campaign to convert the Jews of Castile: "Friar Vincent Ferrer could convert only a few Jews, and the people spitefully put the Jews in Castile to the sword and killed many, and this occurred all over Castile in a single day. . . . Then the Jews themselves came to the churches to be baptized, and so they were; and very many in Castile were made into Christians."[11]

Isolation and Ignorance

Another factor in the relations between religions during the period leading up to the Inquisition was the relative isolation between small towns. Travel was difficult, and the vast majority of citizens rarely ventured farther than the next village. Kamen notes, "Over four-fifths of Spain's population lived . . . beyond the reach of the big towns to which the villagers only went on market days to sell their produce."[12]

Isolated among their own kind and ignorant of other cultures and customs, Spain's rural population grew deeply suspicious of anyone who looked or acted in unfamiliar ways. Wild rumors frequently circulated throughout the countryside. One such rumor blamed the Jews for periodic outbreaks of plague that devastated Spain and the rest of Europe. The plague was described as a Jewish plot to kill Catholics. Significantly smaller numbers of Jews died from plague than Catholics, and this was seen as evidence of such a plot. This may have been due to the Jews' customs; for example, they minimized the risk of infection because they buried their dead quickly and lived in their own neighborhoods, separate from Catholics.

Spaniards in the working classes had another reason to resent minorities: They believed that Jews and Muslims took jobs that rightfully belonged to Catholics. This bitterness had existed for centuries and sometimes broke out in violence. In 1449, for example, mobs of people in Toledo protested a new tax levy by rioting and killing Jews and looting and burning their homes. They incorrectly believed that Jews were behind the new tax simply because they were prominent moneylenders. Still another instance of mob fury occurred in 1454 in the city of Valladolid. A child was robbed and murdered, and by the time it was discovered, the body had been torn apart by dogs. Rumors quickly spread that Jews had ripped out the child's heart, burned it, and then drank wine mingled with the body's ashes. Further rumors asserted that the guilty parties were wealthy and had bribed local judges to dismiss the case. As a result, church authorities continued to rail against the Jews' alleged crimes and heresies. Bernáldez noted:

> They did not believe that God rewarded virginity and chastity;
> their whole aim was to increase and multiply. At the time that this
> heretical depravity arose, many monasteries founded by Gentiles
> and merchants were violated, and many professed nuns were corrupted and mocked, some of them by gifts, others by trickery . . .
> and the *conversos* did it to injure Jesus Christ and the Church.[13]

The Monarchy Steps In

A dramatic turning point in the increasingly tense situation came in 1478, when the Spanish king and queen decided to intervene. Up until this point the rulers had not been particularly hostile toward the Jews (or

Looking Back

Simmering Resentment

Below the surface of the peaceful coexistence between Spain's Catholics, Jews, and Muslims, resentment simmered. In part this was simply due to a general fear of anyone who was different. But there were also specific reasons—notably that many people in the Catholic majority felt that those from minority groups were taking away jobs that should have gone to them. As a result, even when they were tolerated, the country's Muslims and Jews were generally considered second-class citizens. These sentiments created fertile ground for those who wished to "cleanse" Spain of non-Christians. Historian Toby Green comments:

> In Castile Jews often sponsored Christians at their baptisms, while Christians did likewise at Jewish circumcision ceremonies. In the 14th century Christians would bring Muslim friends to mass and even hire Muslim buskers to play music in church during night vigils. . . . Yet in spite of all this sharing in one another's lives, the fault lines between the three faiths were always there, waiting to be exaggerated by extremists.

Toby Green, *Inquisition: The Reign of Fear*. New York: St. Martin's, 2007, pp. 23–24.

the much smaller Muslim minority). On the other hand, Ferdinand and Isabella also had powerful advisors who passionately tried to convince them of the need to get rid of the nation's Jews. One of these advisors was a monk named Alonso de Hojeda. He lived in Seville and had been Isabella's confessor during her childhood in that city. (Confession is the Catholic practice of divulging one's sins to a priest.)

For years de Hojeda had been telling the royal couple wild and unsubstantiated stories. Among other claims, de Hojeda declared—without corroboration or evidence—that Jews poisoned the wells of Christians, desecrated their holy relics, and murdered Christian children and drank their blood. These and other lurid stories helped convince Ferdinand and Isabella of the necessity of cleansing their land of its Jewish population.

Ferdinand and Isabella had two main reasons for agreeing. As pious Catholics they believed that bringing nonbelievers into the church was the right thing to do—that is, they felt an obligation to save the souls of non-Catholics. If Jews refused to convert, it was necessary to expel or execute them in order to cleanse Spain of heretics. At the same time, Ferdinand and Isabella were also shrewd politicians. They recognized that an inquisition could have practical political advantages for them.

Political Advantages

Chief among the political advantages for the monarchs was that an inquisition could solidify their power. Belonging to a single religion would create a bond between their subjects, thus bolstering the king and queen's dream of consolidating the separate kingdoms and ethnic groups of Spain into a single nation. Ferdinand and Isabella's marriage in 1469 had already united their respective kingdoms, Aragon and Castile, into one powerful domain. They were eager to bring the rest of Spain under their control. (These separate kingdoms eventually became modern-day Spain; for clarity, the separate realms are referred to as Spain.)

Related to the goal of uniting Spain was the idea that making it an entirely Catholic nation would reduce the chance of uprisings based on religious differences. Ferdinand and Isabella saw any violence—particularly between Jews and Catholics—as a threat to their power, especially if it escalated into civil war. All in all, the monarchs reasoned, converting all of their subjects to Catholicism was an important goal. Religious scholar Anne W. Carroll comments, "Isabella knew that Spain's unity as a nation depended upon a strong Church—Spain might as well not exist if it were not Christian through and through."[14]

The Pope's Blessing

The king and queen saw that in order to accomplish their political goals they—not the church—needed to control the Inquisition. That way, they could make sure that their political wishes were met. This was an unprecedented idea—in times past, the church had firmly controlled all of Europe's inquisitions.

In order to have the authority to establish their own inquisition, however, Ferdinand and Isabella still needed formal approval from Pope Sixtus IV. Sixtus was resistant, wanting to retain his considerable power and arguing that any inquisitions should be under the control of the church. But the Spanish monarchs forced the issue through political maneuvering. They threatened to withhold military support and money from Sixtus. They knew that he desperately needed this help; he was trying to subdue rebellious nobles and Turkish Muslims who were threatening land that the church controlled. So the pope was forced to submit to Ferdinand and Isabella's demands. Historian Cullen Murphy notes, "In the end, Sixtus stood down . . . effectively [agreeing to] state control over the Inquisition."[15]

In 1478 he issued a declaration, called a papal bull, giving his blessing to the formal establishment of the Spanish Inquisition. The bull specifically granted the authority to seek out *conversos*—Jews who had outwardly converted but continued to practice their religion in secret. Sixtus asserted that these secret Jews caused Spain's problems:

> We are aware that in different cities of your kingdoms of Spain many of those who were regenerated by the sacred baptismal waters of their own free will have returned secretly to the observance of the laws and customs of the Jewish [faith]. . . . Because of the crimes of these men and the tolerance of the Holy See [papal authority] towards them civil war, murder and innumerable ills afflict your kingdoms.[16]

The First Tribunals

Once the pope formally approved Ferdinand and Isabella's plan, the monarchs ordered the creation of a bureaucracy to organize it. The king and queen's official proclamation stated their reasons:

In 1492 the Jews, along with the last of the Muslims, were expelled from Spain. This nineteenth-century lithograph depicts Thomas de Torquemada (center), Spain's inquisitor-general, persuading Queen Isabella to uphold her edict of expulsion despite the pleas of Jewish leaders for her to repeal it.

In our kingdoms there are some bad Christians, both men and women. . . . Although they have been baptised in the True Faith, they bear only the name and appearance of Christians, for they daily return to the superstitions [of the Jews]. . . . Not only have they persisted in their blind and obstinate heresy, but their children and descendants do likewise, and those who treat [deal] with them also are stained by that same infidelity and heresy.[17]

Regulations and procedures for the new tribunals were drawn up. Two Dominican priests, Miguel de Morillo and Juan de San Martin, became the first inquisitors, with two lay assistants to help them. They gathered information and evidence about suspects and held the first tribunal in Seville in September 1480. Bernáldez noted, "They began to sentence people to death by fire. The first time, they took out six men and women to the Plaza La Tablada to be burned, and so they were burned; and Friar Alonso [de Hojeda] from San Pablo (who was zealous for the faith of Jesus Christ, and the one who tried the hardest to get this inquisition in Seville) preached."[18]

The reach of the Inquisition rapidly grew from that. By the end of 1481, nearly three hundred people had been burned in Seville alone. Within a few years the Inquisition established tribunals in several cities besides Seville. At this point a monk named Tomás de Torquemada dominated the Inquisition's activities. Torquemada had been a close spiritual advisor to Isabella during her childhood in Seville, and once Isabella ascended to the throne the degree of his influence rose significantly. By the time the Inquisition was established, his word was highly valued by the monarchs. According to one story, for example, he intervened when a group of wealthy Jews offered to pay Ferdinand a huge sum of money to end the persecution of Jews. Ferdinand was tempted, but the infuriated Torquemada stormed into the royal court. He told the king and queen that, according to the Bible, Judas Iscariot had betrayed Christ for thirty pieces of silver, but that now Ferdinand was thinking of "selling" him for thirty thousand ducats. Thanks at least in part to this fiery display of emotion, Ferdinand decided not to take the offer.

> **WORDS IN CONTEXT**
> **lay**
> Having to do with a person with close connections to the church who is not a priest, nun, or monk.

In 1488 the monarchs named Torquemada the head of the Inquisition. They also established a central council to assist him: the *Consejo de la Suprema y General Inquisición* (Council of the Supreme and General Inquisition), commonly called the *Suprema*. By 1492 the *Suprema* oversaw tribunals in eight cities, and more were added later, including several in Spanish colonies overseas.

Chasing Sin

In its early years the Inquisition restricted itself to exposing *conversos*, as well as Catholics who had fallen away from or spoken against the church. Over time, however, the Inquisition's scope widened to include crimes that were simply viewed as immoral, such as sex between unmarried people, homosexuality, bigamy, and sex with children. Some of these so-called crimes of faith were far-fetched. In northern Spain, for example, horse smuggling was a problem. Corrupt local officials were doing nothing to stop it. The king put the matter into the hands of the *Suprema*, which somehow determined that horse smuggling was a crime of faith and therefore an insult to God.

Ordinary people of all social classes were potential victims of inquisitional tribunals. This included priests, monks, and nuns, all sworn to live by the church's strict rules. These rules included such strictures as remaining celibate—that is, forgoing sex—and living in silence, or poverty. The goal was to avoid the everyday world and its temptations. But sometimes—often, if some accounts are believed—monks and nuns strayed. They appreciated secular (that is, nonreligious) life too much, indulging in such scandalous behavior as taking lovers, enjoying an excess of wine and food, and accepting bribes for favors. Such deviations from the ideal made them ripe targets for the stern judges of the Inquisition.

Several Factors

Many factors went into the making of the Inquisition. Some were the well-established reasons behind persecution that had been used by earlier inquisitions, such as simmering resentment against strangers and minorities. A combination of pious belief and practical politics also convinced the Spanish monarchy to establish the Inquisition as a formal institution that would soon profoundly control the daily life of virtually all Spaniards.

Chapter Two

Old Christians

By the time of the Inquisition, Catholicism had dominated religion—and daily life—for some fifteen hundred years. So it would be difficult to overstate its importance in the lives of Old Christians—those whose families had been Catholic for generations. This was true at every level of society, from kings and queens to soldiers, shopkeepers, farmers, and other everyday people. Writer Erna Paris comments, "To enter the Middle Ages is to step into a God-drenched world."[19]

One measure of how powerfully religion affected daily life was simply the number of churches. Even remote villages had one, and every neighborhood of a larger town had its own. Big cities had beautiful cathedrals, and wealthy families had their own chapels, where they could worship in private. In every case churches were finer and more elaborate than all other buildings.

Church rituals marked milestones from birth to death, such as baptism (the ceremony that welcomed an infant into the fold), marriage, and funeral rites. Social status also depended to a large degree on religion. For example, people who were especially pious—that is, strongly religious—were generally considered superior. This reputation was an advantage when seeking a powerful or prestigious position, such as being on a city council.

Regular attendance at church services, at least weekly and often daily, was taken for granted—and the clergy kept a strict eye on this. Priests scolded those who shirked their religious duties, or worse; everyday people faced punishments such as fines or public whipping for not attending church regularly. Historian James B. Anderson comments, "To show no interest in church affairs . . . was considered a public scandal. [Events such as] important Easter ceremonies were carefully watched to detect who was missing."[20]

Day by Day, Year by Year

On a day-by-day basis, religion affected virtually every hour of a person's work and life. People prayed before eating or sleeping. They ate according to church teachings such as the rule forbidding meat on Fridays. Fishermen had their boats blessed by priests to ensure safety and prosperity. Townspeople marked the hours by listening to church bells, and certain patterns of the bells told them when to pray. And those same church bells alerted them to dangers such as fire or approaching raiders.

Old Christians also marked the days of the year through observances such as holidays and feast days. Chief among these were Christmas and Easter, but there were many others, such as the feast days that honored individual saints of the church. Furthermore, religion also bound a community socially. One example concerned guilds, organizations formed by craftsmen for mutual aid. Each guild chose a particular saint to act as its

The Church of San Jeronimo el Real (St. Jerome the Royal Church) was one of numerous Gothic churches built in Spain after the country's unification in the fifteenth century. Completed in 1505, for centuries it has been the church where the prince/princess of Asturias, heir to the Spanish throne, is invested.

guardian, and the feast days of those patron saints were cause for celebration, parades, and rituals.

The Lives of the Clergy

Ordinary people such as guild members were typically pious, but of course (at least officially) so were members of the clergy, most of them monks or nuns who ranked relatively low in the church hierarchy. They had a wide range of lifestyles. These differed according to their particular orders— that is the formalized group they belonged to, such as the Franciscans or Dominicans. For example, some orders took vows of poverty. Some cut themselves off from the rest of the world, living in convents (for nuns) or monasteries (for monks) and devoting themselves to learning and prayer. They dressed simply, ate simply, and led daily lives largely devoted to the labor required to maintain the monasteries or convents where they lived, such as working in kitchens or maintaining libraries and vineyards. Some orders cut themselves off from the world completely. But others were devoted to work in the everyday world, such as providing help for the needy and shelter for travelers. No matter what order they belonged to, the daily routines of monks and nuns were punctuated by regular and frequent sessions of group or individual prayer.

For an Old Christian, being a monk or nun was a common and honorable way to live. Many young men from poor families entered monasteries because they knew they were guaranteed regular meals. And refuge from the outside world could mean a satisfying life of religious contemplation. One monk of the period wrote, "Happy the humble state of the scholar who retires from this malicious world and there in the pleasant countryside, with modest table and dwelling, governs his life with God alone, and passes his days all by himself, neither envied nor envying."[21]

But not everything about being a monk was as sweet. For example, one common characteristic of monks, no matter what order they were in, was an aversion to cleanliness—they rarely bathed. This was true for the general populace as well, and it stood in sharp contrast to the practices of Jews and Muslims. According to the precepts of their religions, Jews and Muslims were scrupulously clean at all times—something that clearly

Looking Back

Objecting to a New Inquisition

There had been occasional trials of heretics before the Spanish Inquisition came into being, but these had been scattered and sporadic. As a result, for many years official persecution had been dormant—that is, inactive. Some Old Christians as well as *conversos* then opposed the resurgence of a new, highly organized and nationwide inquisition. In some cases this opposition was due to moral outrage, because Old Christians felt it was wrong to persecute heretics so harshly. In other cases it was because these Old Christians simply did not appreciate the government meddling in their affairs. Historian Henry Charles Lea comments on this, using as an example inquisitional courts (*córtes*) in the city of Tarazona:

> Thus far the people had been passive; they had accepted the action of the Córtes of Tarazona, apparently under the impression that the new Inquisition would be as inert as the old had so long been, but, as they awoke to the reality, an opposition arose which called a halt and [the city] never celebrated another auto[-da-fé]. Not only the Conversos but many of the Old Christians denounced the Inquisition as contrary to the liberties of the land. The chief objections urged against it were the secrecy of procedure and the confiscation of estates.

Henry Charles Lea, *A History of the Inquisition of Spain*, vol. 1. New York: Macmillan, 1922. www.gutenberg.org.

marked them as non-Catholics. Anderson writes, "Spanish monks, according to their practice of establishing principles opposite to the infidel [nonbeliever], considered physical dirt as the test of moral purity and true faith. By dining and sleeping year in and year out in the same unchanged woolen frock, they arrived at the height of their ambition—the odor of sanctity [holiness]."[22]

Careful and Discreet Disagreement

Most monks shared the Inquisition's general belief that converting or punishing heretics was necessary. And overall, so did the population at large. Beginning long before the period of the Inquisition, a majority of Spain's Old Christians approved of converting minorities, by force or threat if necessary. On the other hand, some Old Christians likely took little notice of such attitudes. For peasants, who made up the vast majority of Spaniards, life was hard, and the struggle to survive likely left even the most devout little time for worry over the nation's religious purity or saving the souls of anyone but themselves.

But some Old Christians did not accept all of the church's supposedly infallible teachings. For example, a writer of the period quotes a man who asserted in 1539 that "there is no heaven, purgatory or hell; at the end we all have to end up in the same place, the bad will go to the same place as the good and the good will go to the same place as the bad."[23] And some people frankly denied the validity of the Inquisition.

But making such comments in public carried the risk of danger, since dissent could easily result in punishment. So opinions had to be voiced carefully and discreetly. One example of someone who was not discreet was a farmer in Galicia who complained that the practice of tithing (donating part of one's income to the church) came not from God but from the church—that is, it had a human origin, not a divine one. This dissent earned him a trial and a conviction of heresy. He was ordered, as Anderson notes, "to

> **WORDS IN CONTEXT**
> **purgatory**
> In Catholicism, a middle state between life and an afterlife in heaven or hell.

31

retract his statement before the church congregation and pay a fine . . . and then was banished from the village as a troublemaker."[24]

Indifference and Ignorance

In some isolated regions of Spain, ancient religious superstitions—such as those about ghosts, the evil eye, black magic, and the power of amulets—had a far stronger influence than did conventional Catholicism. In such cases the intrusion of the Inquisition, the royal government, and conventional religion in general were deeply suspect and openly rejected.

Frequently, monks (usually traveling in pairs) moved through the countryside to try to convince local residents—many of whom still clung to ancient religions—to accept Catholicism. They typically used a variety of impressive techniques to drive their messages home. Anderson writes, "To impress and frighten the audience, various kinds of theatrical devices were used, simulating the flames and screams of the condemned souls in hell, highlighted by grisly skulls among sulfurous fumes. The torrid speeches awakened the attention of the most dimwitted, and the scenes of hell made the women swoon."[25]

But the locals were often not convinced, which was a source of great frustration for the church. The missionaries were also resented simply because they were foreigners. For example, the chief inquisitor for the mountainous Basque country of northern Spain complained that he and his colleagues were scorned because they could not speak the local Basque language. He noted, "We are hated as officials of the Holy Church, especially in this town."[26]

And clergy were often dismayed not only by the indifference or suspicion but also by the simple ignorance even among those who were already believers. For example, in 1554 Felipe de Meneses, a monk in the region of Castile, complained about the lack of religious education among people he encountered, whether in the tiniest villages or the largest cities. He wrote, "In every two words they will utter three errors or heresies, though in reality those are not heresies but idiocies and foolishness. . . . Out of three hundred residents, you will find barely thirty who know what any ordinary Christian is obliged to know."[27]

Monks were members of the regular clergy who resided in monasteries and lived in accordance with the rules established for their particular order. This fresco portrays a monk commemorating the biblical miracle where after blessing only five loaves of bread and two fish, Jesus was able to feed five thousand people.

Resistance

At the same time, some Old Christians went beyond dissent or indifference, defying the Inquisition's extreme measures. They typically did so out of compassion for other humans and a belief that one religion is not superior to another. As a Catholic man in Castile asked in 1501, "Who knows which is the better religion, ours or those of the Muslims and Jews?"[28]

As a result, a relatively small but significant number of Old Christians actively resisted the Inquisition. Historians stress that the entire country was by no means aflame with a desire to root out heresy. Rather, a relatively small group of radical extremists was responsible for the Inquisition, and these religious fanatics remained powerful only through the support of the king and queen. Henry Kamen comments, "Spain was not, as often imagined, a society dominated exclusively by zealots."[29]

Dissenters had to be careful about speaking out in public, with the danger of exposure and thus punishment always present. But there were other ways in which Old Christians could secretly defy the Inquisition. One was to hide potential victims or help them flee the country. For example, Pedro de Torres, an Old Christian in the city of Ciudad Real, hid eight *conversos* in his home during a riot in 1474 and likely saved their lives. These were brave acts, since the Old Christians knew that anyone found guilty of aiding suspects would, like the suspects themselves, face severe consequences.

Within the Catholic clergy there were even occasional admissions of doubt about the Inquisition's actions. In 1551 a Jesuit priest expressed his reservations (in secret) to another priest: "It is a great pity that there seems nobody willing to leave these poor people anywhere to stay on earth, and I would like to have the energy to become their defender, particularly since one encounters among them more virtue than among the Old Christians and *hidalgos* [Spanish nobility]."[30]

Teruel

Ferdinand and Isabella were not among those who expressed any doubt, at least publicly, about the work of the Inquisition. The monarchy was eager to quash any resistance. This was perhaps especially true when it concerned the nobility, who controlled regions of Spain, or anyone else in a position of power. In 1484 Ferdinand and Isabella issued a blanket statement:

> Therefore we say, charge, and order you—under the risk of incurring our anger, indignation, a penalty of 10,000 gold florins, and

In Their Own Words

The Pope's Condemnation

Within a few years of the start of the Inquisition, Pope Sixtus IV became aware of reports of the institution's excesses against accused heretics. He was particularly concerned about Old Christians—especially wealthy ones whose fortunes could be seized. In 1482 Sixtus issued a statement on the subject, which included this passage:

> [The Inquisition] has for some time been moved not by zeal for the faith and the salvation of souls, but by lust for wealth, and many true and faithful Christians, on the testimony of enemies, rivals, slaves, and other lower and even less proper persons have without any legitimate proof been thrust into secular [lay] prisons, tortured and condemned as heretics, and deprived of their goods and property and handed over to the secular arm to be executed, to the peril of souls, setting a pernicious [wicked] example, and causing disgust to many.

Quoted in Henry Kamen, *The Spanish Inquisition*. London: Weidenfeld and Nicolson, 1965, p. 34.

the deprivation of your office if the contrary is done by you or any of your retinue—that you honor and recognize each one of the inquisitors and other inquisitorial officials and agents, according to their rank, estate, and condition. We further order you to give them all the help and assistance they need and request whenever they require it. . . . Refrain from doing the opposite in any way, and do not consent or allow the opposite to be done, to the extent that my favor is dear to you, and that you do not wish to incur my anger, indignation, and the aforesaid penalty.[31]

Despite this royal order, some local authorities resisted the Inquisition. The city of Teruel in Aragon was a prominent example of an entire community of Old Christians that did so, when its most distinguished citizens banded together to oppose the government. They did not necessarily object to the Inquisition's goal. They simply hated the idea of the king telling them what to do.

In 1483 the Inquisition tried to establish a regional tribunal in the city, despite Teruel's long history of defending itself against outsiders and government control. When the inquisitors came to the city, its leaders met them at the protective walls that surrounded it. Paris notes, "The notables of Teruel lined up behind the gates of their city, and when the inquisitors, Juan Colivera and Martin Navarro, arrived in a cloud of road dust, they bluntly refused them entry. Enraged, the priests retreated to the nearby village of Cella where they plotted what to do next."[32]

The inquisitors were fully prepared for their work, according to the city's historian, with an array of "executioners, weapons, and nooses."[33] Nonetheless, Teruel's leaders chose to avoid armed resistance. This was a wise decision, since the king could have raised a large army against them. Instead, they relied on the force of negotiation and a planned legal challenge.

They appointed a young man named Gonzalo Ruiz to represent the town in a series of negotiations. His initial talks confirmed the intruders' intentions. Ruiz reported back that the church's representatives were "coming to conduct the Inquisition with the same disorder they inflicted [elsewhere], bringing with them the selfsame regulations, unfair and contrary to all law."[34] The city fathers then insisted that the inquisitorial representatives stay outside the city's walls. The intruders were forced to settle in a monastery some distance away. As the standoff continued, the inquisitors tried to force their way in by threatening to excommunicate the entire town, but they failed to get formal approval for this from Rome. The negotiations dragged on, and after two years Ferdinand himself was obliged to step in. He wrote a fiery letter to the city fathers, stating that their resistance had increased "the anger and displeasure that we have toward you for having so dishonestly and so without cause prohibited the inquisitors of heretical depravity from entering your city to carry out the inquisition." The letter went on to say, "Our unchangeable

Monks were generally selected to accompany chained heretics condemned to be burned at the stake by order of the Court of the Inquisition (pictured).

will is that the inquisitors shall enter that city and be received peacefully along with their agents. We now explicitly order you to go out personally into the road and to peacefully bring that inquisitor and his agents into your city. . . . They shall exercise all the mercy and piety that the law and good conscience allow."[35]

Ferdinand sent an emissary to the Vatican, the home of the pope and the center of the church. This emissary succeeded in obtaining the right of the inquisitors to enter the city. In 1485 the city finally surrendered. The inquisitional representatives were able to set up a tribunal within the city walls without violence.

The Edict of Grace

The establishment of this tribunal was typical of how the inquisitional process operated in general. It began when officials arrived in a town and issued a proclamation called the Edict of Grace. This announcement was typically made at Sunday Mass when everyone was in church. The Edict of Grace had two purposes. One was to offer a period (usually thirty to forty days) in which people could confess their own heretical thoughts or deeds. If they did, they would be "reconciled"—that is, brought back into the fold of the church. Furthermore, they would be treated gently and guaranteed exemption from serious punishment. The Edict read, in part:

> Those who come to confess shall be given penances that are healthful for their souls; they shall not receive a penalty of death or perpetual prison, and their goods shall not be taken or disturbed for the crimes they confess, inasmuch as it pleases their Highnesses to treat mercifully those who come to truly reconcile themselves during the edict of grace. Those who seek such reconciliation shall be received into union with the Holy Mother Church.[36]

One example of this "free" confession dates from 1545, when in the village of Aboler a man named Diego de Almodovar confessed to excessive gambling—and that he swore when he lost. De Almodovar stated:

> Sometimes . . . I said with anger and passion, "I don't believe in so-and-so," or "I deny so-and-so," for which I ask pardon from God

and a beneficial penance from your lordships. . . . Now I have heard that your lordships have ordered edicts published and read in which many things are said about such matters, and I have been informed that I cannot be absolved of this sin unless I come to declare it before your lordships, on account of which I beg you to treat me mercifully.[37]

A Network of Informants

But the Edict of Grace had another purpose beyond free confession. It also encouraged people to report on others they suspected of wrongdoing. In each region, this created a network of informants, with people reporting neighbors or even family members they suspected of anti-Catholic behavior. Eager to support and capitalize on this spy network, the church developed a number of guidelines on how to identify suspects. For example, the officials advised the public that when seeking out Jews, people should be aware of certain clues, based primarily on Jewish religious rituals:

> **WORDS IN CONTEXT**
> **edict**
> An official proclamation.

> If you see that your neighbors are wearing clean and fancy clothes on Saturdays, they are Jews. If they clean their houses on Fridays and light candles earlier than usual on that night, they are Jews. If they eat unleavened bread and begin their meals with celery and lettuce during Holy Week, they are Jews. If they say prayers facing a wall, bowing back and forth, they are Jews.[38]

During the period of the Inquisition, some Old Christians privately disapproved of the Inquisition, and a few openly defied it. Others were simply uninterested or ignorant. But most Old Christians were at least somewhat sympathetic to its goals and methods, and many actively supported it by spying on and denouncing suspected heretics. This support augmented the spread of the Inquisition and helped make it a firmly established part of Spain's daily life.

Chapter Three

To Be a Jew or Muslim in Spain

As the Inquisition's influence grew, restrictions for minorities increased, and many Jews and Muslims chose to convert to Christianity. This was not new in Spain; some families had generations before chosen to convert as a way of easing relations with Catholic neighbors and business partners. But once the Inquisition began, this phenomenon exploded; hundreds of thousands of Jews and Muslims underwent baptism, the ceremony that welcomed them into the Catholic Church.

To complete the transition, the *conversos*, or New Christians, gave up their former religious practices and fervently embraced Catholicism. For example, they abandoned traditional dietary laws such as avoiding pork, a law shared by both Jews and Muslims. Instead, they observed such Catholic practices as not eating meat on Fridays. Also, Jewish *conversos* no longer circumcised their boys, as Jewish law dictated, and no longer avoided work on Saturday, the holiest day of the week for Jews. Furthermore, many converts changed their surnames to ones that were not suggestive of Judaism. Some *converso* families even sent their firstborn sons into the Catholic priesthood to demonstrate their sincerity.

Despite such changes, the New Christians were still generally seen as second-class citizens and denied many privileges. For example, they were forbidden (with rare exceptions) to own land or hire Catholic employees. A set of regulations drawn up in 1627 by Gaspar Isidro de Argüello, a senior member of the Inquisition, outlined other regulations:

> Because those reconciled individuals must perform and complete their penances with humility, and feel the pain of their errors, the

inquisitors must order them not to possess public offices or . . . be advocates, landlords, apothecaries, spice dealers, physicians or surgeons, or [medical] bleeders or public criers. They may not carry gold, silver, coral, pearls, or other things, nor precious stones; they may not wear any sort of silk or camlet [a type of fine cloth]. . . . They may not ride horses or carry arms their entire lives, under penalty of falling into relapse.[39]

Estimates vary widely, but as many as 600,000 Jews and 250,000 Muslims may have taken this route by the end of the fifteenth century. Publicly renouncing one's faith was a radical step, and almost always not a welcome one for minorities. But as the Inquisition tightened its grip, conversion often provided the only path to survival. Historian John Edward Longhurst writes, "They chose baptism as a lesser evil than death."[40]

The Working Life

One area in which minorities, even those who converted, suffered was in their working life. In this respect, conversion did not always shield them from persecution. Before the Inquisition, Jews had typically held jobs such as merchants, doctors, or artisans (such as textile makers). In particular, many Jews had occupations related to finance, such as rent or tax collectors and money lending (because Catholic religious law forbade money lending).

Before the Inquisition, *conversos* holding such occupations were tolerated by the Catholic majority. But during the Inquisition, even *conversos* who sincerely embraced Catholicism were never welcomed fully into Spanish society. They were often subjected to petty and humiliating incidents of discrimination. For example, when the inquisitional tribunal in the town of Longroño needed to appoint an official physician, no suitable Old Christian could be found. The tribunal was forced to ask for special permission from the *Suprema* to hire a *converso* physician named Dr. Béles. The *Suprema* ruled that the doctor could be consulted—but only if it were done without recognition of his title.

Despite their general status as second-class citizens, a handful of *con-*

It was a violation of canon (Church) law for Christians to lend money to other Christians and charge interest on the loans. Therefore, wealthy Jewish bankers were brought into Christian communities to serve as moneylenders and tax collectors. This oil painting on a wooden panel depicts a banking couple tallying pieces of gold and silver.

versos—virtually all of them Jews—played significant roles in Spanish society and government. For example, Francisco Lopez Villalobos, a *converso*, was Ferdinand's court physician. Two other prominent *conversos* were Abraham Seneor and Gabriel Sanchez, top financial advisors to the king and queen. (It was Sanchez who financed Christopher Columbus's famous voyage to the New World.) Historian Henry Charles Lea writes of the royal couple's financial advisors, "The treasuries of the kingdoms were virtually in their hands, and it was their skill in organizing the supplies that rendered practicable the enterprises of [royalty]."[41]

In some ways the working life was better in towns or cities than in the countryside. Even uneducated Jews and Muslims who came from outside the cities had better chances of finding relatively good work, such as being servants to wealthy Catholic families or holding minor positions in small manufacturing operations such as blacksmithing. But work for minorities was still limited—and some Christians asserted that Jews and Muslims who could not find work had only themselves to blame. Andrés Bernáldez wrote at the time:

> Most of them [Jews] were usurers [moneylenders] who had many artful ways and tricks, because they all supported themselves from leisurely sorts of work, and in buying and selling they had no conscience where Christians were concerned. They never wanted to take jobs that involved plowing or digging, or walking through the fields guarding flocks, nor did they teach their children [to do so]; rather, they took work in town, which involved sitting down and earning something to eat with little effort.[42]

Work for Muslims

In general, Jews had better chances for middle-class occupations than Muslims did. In part this was because Jewish culture had always placed a strong emphasis on education, giving them an advantage in the job market. The situation was much different for Muslims, however. Islamic culture and scholarship had once been strong. During the so-called Islamic Golden Age, which lasted roughly from the mid-seventh century to the mid-thirteenth century, the major centers of Islamic culture (including the Spanish city of Cordova) were centers of innovation in such areas as medicine, philosophy, and mathematics. Cullen Murphy comments, "In its golden age, Islamic Spain was among the most civilized places on the planet—renowned for its scientists and philosophers, artists and architects, poets and musicians."[43]

But this slowly changed. In part this was because of invaders from outside who destabilized the Islamic Empire. By the time of the Inquisition, Muslims in Spain were isolated from their once-strong realm and lived as second-class citizens, unable to maintain their culture's once-high level of education or to rise beyond menial labor. This work in-

Looking Back

A Midnight Visit

For a New Christian who had been denounced, a visit from the security arm of the Inquisition was a terrifying event. These officers typically carried out their arrests of suspects at night, taking them away without explanation. In this passage, writer Erna Paris describes a typical arrest and the fear it inspired:

> A knock on the door at the still hour of midnight. Scuffling noises, denials, cries for help. The victim is led away. His or her property is scrupulously inventoried. Children are abandoned in the street unless they are taken in by others. No one will see the victim again until the day of his or her sentencing. . . . Family members shrink from one another, including from small children who might innocently reveal what has gone on in their homes. Every night when darkness falls parents clasp their children to them and creep from the city, crouched shadowy figures furtively hugging the sides of roads.

Erna Paris, *The End of Days*. Amherst, NY: Prometheus, 1995, pp. 162–63.

cluded farm labor such as harvesting olives and oranges, shepherding and woodcutting, or hauling resources like timber for shipbuilding. Some peasants—especially Muslims—were *journaleros*, migrant laborers who traveled from region to region to plant or harvest crops.

For Muslims there were occasional but rare exceptions to such restrictions on where and how they could work. For example, their supposed wickedness could be overlooked when it was useful. In one such instance, Ferdinand's armies became short on gunpowder, the making of which was a traditional occupation for Muslims. So the monarch removed certain restrictive employment laws, ensuring that Muslims would be free to manufacture the explosive.

Ghettos

Besides work, another major restriction for urban Jews and Muslims centered on where they could live. Minorities were restricted to separate areas, which in the case of Jews were called ghettos (in Spanish, *aljamas*). Such restrictions existed before the Inquisition arose but now dramatically increased—to the point that many Jews and Muslims ventured only rarely outside their own neighborhoods. Sometimes these separate areas were walled, with gates that were locked at night. And minorities often were not allowed to own land inside the walls, instead renting from Catholic landlords.

There were exceptions—for example, on occasion Jewish doctors were allowed to leave ghettos at night to tend to Catholic families. And in some cities residential restrictions were simply ignored. For example, in Valladolid *conversos* could own houses, land, and vineyards wherever they liked.

Ghettos, although restrictive, were not necessarily shabby. For example, Seville's ghetto, Barrio Santa Cruz, was a neighborhood of narrow, well-kept streets crowded with homes, shops, synagogues, and small factories for goldsmiths, jewelers, and other artisans. And since a number of *conversos* were relatively prosperous, ghettos such as this one included elegant homes and small, pleasant squares lined with orange trees.

Escaping or Staying

Clearly, there were many advantages to becoming a New Christian. But not all members of minorities chose to convert, feeling instead that it was more important to remain true to their religion. So some fled to other countries such as England, where their lives would be less restrictive. Some Muslims and Jews tried to move within Spain, since some cities were more tolerant than others. But this did not always work. An

A. L'ECOLE.

Throughout most of the Middle Ages, the Muslim world promoted schooling for boys and consequently evolved into one of the leading centers of art, knowledge and scholarship in the West. However, Muslim intellectual prominence was eclipsed by the Renaissance and Scientific Revolution in Western Europe.

eyewitness to the flight of Jews from the city of Cordova following a period of violence recalled, "Of those who escaped, many went to the town
of Palma. Others went to Ecija and Jerez and anywhere else they could
secure refuge from the local governors. In Adamtu and in Montoro and
in La Rambla they were robbed and severely manhandled. In Almodovar
del Campo some of the Conversos were robbed and killed."[44]

Those who refused to convert and chose to stay in their homes risked
danger. One such person was Judah Benardut, a Jew who lived in the
town of Calatayud. In about 1470, when asked why he did not convert,
Benardut replied, "I do not wish to become a Christian neither for hon-
ours nor in order to escape insults. I hold fast to my religion and I believe
that I will be saved in it, and the more humiliations I have to endure to
sustain my religion the more shall my soul be saved."[45]

Crypto-Jews and Crypto-Muslims

Still other minority members chose another route, one fraught with
greater danger than all other options. These Jews and Muslims converted to Christianity but secretly kept their native religions. These secret worshippers are known as crypto-Jews and crypto-Muslims. (The
prefix *crypto-* refers to something that is se-
cret or hidden). Old Christians of the time
had other names for them: secret Jews were
marranos (an insulting slang term meaning
"pig"); their Muslim counterparts were typically referred to simply as *moriscos*, the same
term used for converted Muslims in general.

Crypto-Jews and crypto-Muslims publicly celebrated major life events such as wed-
dings in Catholic churches. They professed
their acceptance of Jesus Christ as the Messiah, the Son of God (which
is not part of Jewish or Islamic belief). But this was simply a front. At
home, for example, Jews observed the weekly Sabbath, the holy day of
rest on Saturday. They also took ritual baths and always wore clean clothing, neither of which was common practice among Catholics at the time.

> **WORDS IN CONTEXT**
>
> *marrano*
>
> A derogatory slang
> word for a Jew who has
> outwardly converted to
> Christianity but prac-
> tices Judaism in secret.

Erna Paris writes, "There was a secret room in [every Jewish] house where the Sabbath table was laid with a clean, white cloth and candles were lit, and hamin [a traditional stew] was served."[46]

Secret Muslims used similar ruses. For example, they adopted common Christian names when in public but referred to themselves by their Muslim names in private. They attended Catholic Mass, but they were able to evade other rituals in various ways. For example, if someone in a crypto-Muslim family was dying, family members could prevent a Catholic priest from attending the dying person by telling him that he had arrived too late.

Danger at Every Turn

But the secret practice of Judaism or Islam was a terribly dangerous game. Fear of discovery dominated every moment of daily life. Every person (outside the immediate family and a trusted circle of friends) was a potential enemy who could bring about the Inquisition's scrutiny. There are many examples of such exposure that led to punishment. In one case in 1597, a man was sentenced to years of imprisonment and the confiscation of his property simply because he was seen bathing.

Women were not exempt from the danger of exposure. In some ways women were more protected from danger than men, since they typically spent less time outside their homes. But they were still vulnerable if they were suspected and reported by neighbors or people who employed them. If accused, these women often invented elaborate stories to explain suspicious behavior. For example, in Toledo in the 1570s a Catholic family noticed that their cook, ostensibly a *converso*, did not eat pork and that she handled the meat with a cloth when preparing meals for the household. Her explanation was that she did not eat pork because it upset her stomach, and she handled it with a cloth because it made her hands smell bad. Despite her explanations she was arrested and, under torture, confessed to secretly observing Judaism.

Looking Back

Separated from Their Past

Conversos in Spain were sometimes shunned by unconverted Jews, who condemned their rejection of their culture and religion. And they were sometimes shunned by Old Christians as well, who still considered them second-class citizens and never fully accepted them. In this passage, historian Norman Roth argues that New Christians were not necessarily troubled by this double rejection—until persecution forced them to reconsider.

> The rejection by Jews certainly did not disturb the conversos, for they considered themselves in fact to be true Christians and totally separated from Jewish society, for the most part. However, the increasing jealousy and then open persecution of the conversos by "old Christians," i.e. Christians by birth, became a major problem. At last, in the mid-fifteenth century, this gave rise to actual open warfare between the "old" and the "new" Christians. Kings were involved; armies fought; certain modern weapons of war were used for the first time; cities were besieged.

Norman Roth, *Conversos, Inquisition, and the Expulsion of the Jews from Spain*. Madison: University of Wisconsin Press, 2002, p. xi.

Another example dates from 1591, when a Catholic woman noticed her neighbor putting clean linen on her husband's corpse—a clear indication that she was a secret Muslim. The accused woman was arrested and tried, but she escaped with only a fine. Another woman called before a tribunal defended herself against accusations of breaking a Catholic law that prohibited eating meat on Fridays by asserting:

I state, Reverend Fathers, that once on a Friday—it happened to me innocently—without thinking that it was Friday, I told my girl to cook a piece of meat that was left over. After I had arranged everything, my husband sent the same girl out to buy fish, and he ordered me to cook it. I said to him, "Why do we need fish on a meat day?" And he answered, "How can you say this is a meat day when it is Friday?" Then he saw the pot with the meat on the fire, and took it off and threw it all out. He was very irritable about it. I told him I had done it innocently, without thinking what day it was.[47]

And still another example concerned a woman in Ciudad Real who in 1513 was accused of being a secret Jew. One accuser said the woman had been observed performing the Jewish ritual of lighting candles on a Friday evening before sunset. According to the official records of her trial, the accuser stated, among other denunciations, "On those Friday nights, María González, Diego de Teva's wife, lit two clean oil lamps with new wicks two hours before it was dark. She adorned and cleaned her house, and adorned it on those Friday nights out of esteem for the Law of Moses."[48] In this case the accused woman did not escape serious punishment—she was convicted and burned at the stake.

> **WORDS IN CONTEXT**
> **denunciation**
> A public accusation, such as declaring that someone has made heretical statements.

Resistance

Increasingly concerned about such events, Jews in many cities across Spain held meetings to discuss the worsening situation. Some who spoke at these meetings advocated becoming or continuing to be *conversos*, feeling that this was the best way to survive. But others advocated armed resistance. A witness to one such meeting recalled hearing comments such as these: "What do you think of them [Catholics] acting thus against us? Are we not the most propertied members of this city, and well loved by the people? Let us collect men together. And if they come to take us, we, together with armed men and the people will

A woodcut depicting the torture and burning in Granada, Spain, of Jews accused of heresy and witchcraft by the Spanish Inquisition. In March 1492, Ferdinand and Isabella issued the Edict of Expulsion requiring Jews—as well as Muslims—to convert to Christianity, leave Spain, or face certain death.

rise up and slay them and so be revenged against our enemies."[49]

According to some sources, in 1486 at least one group of Jews began plotting just such an uprising. According to this story, an alliance of prominent Jews in Seville planned to assassinate several inquisitors. They succeeded in killing one, but the rest of the plan was not completed. This was because the daughter of one of the conspirators told her lover, an Old Christian, about the plot. The lover reported them to the tribunal, which rounded up the conspirators, convicted them, and burned them at the stake. Because of her role in exposing the plot, the daughter was spared.

One plot that did succeed was the murder in 1485 of a priest named Pedro de Arbués. De Arbués was a leading inquisitional figure in the city of Zaragoza, well known for his devotion to his faith and to strictly following the regulations of the Inquisition. According to a sixteenth-century historian, "He took strength in the exact observance of the rules

. . . and was an example to all his colleagues. He divided his time between study and prayer . . . and mortified [punished] his body with harsh whips in order to strengthen his virtue."[50]

Many residents of Zaragoza, not just Jews, resented the Inquisition's presence there. They considered it an intrusion by the royal court on city affairs. So de Arbués knew he had enemies in town and habitually wore a steel cap and a suit of protective armor under his robes. Despite these precautions, he was stabbed to death while at prayer in Zaragoza's main cathedral. Suspicion quickly fell on a group of prominent *converso* families, and the event became a rallying point for anti-Semitic feeling. In the trials following de Arbués's murder, some thirty *conversos* were executed or harshly punished for their alleged roles in the crime.

Although it was never proved, it is certainly possible that a conspiracy of converts did kill the priest. However, this would have gone against the usual pattern of resistance. Generally, *conversos* avoided violence in favor of fighting the Inquisition in other ways, such as bringing lawsuits that challenged discriminatory laws and policies. Another way in which New Christians could mount legal challenges was to become politically influential. For example, in several urban centers they became members of the city council. Not surprisingly, many Old Christians resented these intrusions. A historian of the time, Diego de Valera, said that in Cordova "there was great enmity and rivalry, since the New Christians were very rich and kept buying public offices, which they made use of so arrogantly that the Old Christians would not put up with it."[51]

Moriscos

Much less is known about Muslims, both converted and secret, than about their Jewish counterparts, in large part because these *moriscos* made up a much smaller group. Only an estimated twelve thousand Muslims were brought to trial for heresy by the Inquisition—a significant number, but far lower than that of the Jews. So they were not examined as closely by the Inquisition. Furthermore, the majority of Muslims were illiterate and poor, so as marginalized figures in society, they warranted virtually no written accounts of their daily lives.

One thing that is clear is that discrimination against Muslims was especially bad in the south, where Spain's Muslim population was concentrated. Like the Jews, they were typically characterized as repulsive enemies of Catholicism. Toby Green writes, "Numerous chroniclers created stereotypes of [Muslims] as ugly, abnormal, different. Slowly, people had come to see . . . Spain's Muslim population in this light. Slowly, the groundwork had been laid for the [Muslims'] destruction."[52]

Furthermore, *moriscos* were generally less vocal than *conversos* in protesting discrimination and persecution. There were several reasons for this. For one, they simply had less incentive. Muslims were typically not persecuted as harshly as Jews, in part because they lived more separate lives, did not interact with Catholics as much, and remained relatively detached from mainstream society. Muslims thus posed less of a threat to Catholics, and the Inquisition did not investigate them as thoroughly as it did the Jewish population.

Another factor, education, may also have played a role in keeping Muslims from pursuing legal action. By the time of the Inquisition, the once formidable academic standards of Islam had fallen in Spain, accompanied by a similar drop in status and wealth. Muslims often lived in lower-class and/or rural communities, and literacy was rare. As a result, overall they lacked the level of wealth, education, and experience needed to mount effective legal campaigns.

The Jews and Muslims of Spain had severely limited options. They could convert to Christianity and abandon all practice of their native faith, they could convert and in public live as Catholics while practicing their own religions in private, they could choose not to convert, or they could flee. All those who chose to remain in Spain, regardless of which route they took, were subject to the whims of a small but powerful group of people: the bureaucracy that operated the Inquisition.

Chapter Four

The Inquisitors

In both scope and size, the Spanish Inquisition was a radical change from inquisitions in Europe's past. It was also very different in how it was organized. Earlier inquisitions had been relatively disorganized, spontaneous, and sporadic events, and they had been under the control of only the church. In contrast, the Spanish version was highly developed, systematic, and run by the government of a nation—the only inquisition ever to fall under direct control of royalty.

In many ways the Spanish Inquisition resembled any well-run business. It had many of the advantages of such an organization, such as the ability to expand its operations as new opportunities arose. But at the same time it also had many of the same problems faced by any business. For example, it had to create and maintain efficient channels between its various levels, smoothly communicating policies and decisions from its top executives to its lower branches. The Inquisition faced other problems common to businesses as well. Historian Robin Vose writes, "Inquisitions were . . . mundane corporate entities, struggling like all such bodies to efficiently make and execute policy while staying more or less within a budget."[53]

Like any large corporation, the Inquisition needed to employ a huge number of individuals who filled a wide range of positions. It needed executive directors, middle managers, administrators, secretaries, economists, legal aides, record keepers, and security officers. In short, the Inquisition was an expansive and largely faceless bureaucratic body. These people carried out the organization's daily tasks, ensuring its smooth operation. Vose comments, "Like all powerful institutions, inquisitions functioned in the final analysis thanks to the efforts of individuals. These ranged from a more or less centralized leadership to local judge-inquisitors, advisors, jailers and armed associates who carried out the bulk of a tribunal's day-to-day activities."[54]

Alphonso de Spina

Many individuals played crucial roles in the Spanish Inquisition. One of the most prominent was a Franciscan monk, Alphonso de Spina. De Spina's main role in the Inquisition stems from a fiery call for the extermination of heretics that he wrote in the mid-1400s. This document, *Fortalitium Fidei* (Latin for "Stronger Faith"), became a cornerstone of the Inquisition's philosophy. It repeated, without evidence, many of the lurid claims that had been made about the wickedness of Jews. A writer for *The Jewish Encyclopedia* notes, "Whatever the enemies of the Jews had written or recounted he presented as truth."[55]

Little is known about the life of de Spina, but it is certain that he was a member of the Franciscan order, a religious scholar, and a top administrator at the University of Salamanca in Castile. Aside from his devotion to prayer and meditation, he delivered sermons, served the poor, and like other clergymen of his stature, wrote scholarly texts. He also served as a confessor to Queen Isabella's half brother, King Henry IV of Castile.

De Spina's life was devoted to the cause of eradicating heresy. He saw himself and his fellow monks and priests as the means to root out nonbelievers. In a letter to another clergyman, he articulated this opinion when he stormed, "And now we—who occupy the places of the saints here on earth and who should be an example of light to the world—see the unbelievers growing and heretics destroying and subverting the Faith of Jesus Christ while we sit silently by."[56]

Torquemada

But de Spina was not the most important figure of the Inquisition. That distinction goes to the Dominican monk who had long been a close advisor to the monarchy: Tomás de Torquemada, whose ruthlessness as the Inquisition's first supreme leader set the tone for the organization as a whole.

Tomás de Torquemada (holding a crucifix) was the infamous Dominican monk appointed grand inquisitor by the Spanish Crown. Torquemada was a major influence in persuading Ferdinand and Isabella to expel the Jews from Spain in 1492.

Torquemada was born in 1420 in the city of Valladolid in Castile. When he was a young man, Torquemada entered the Dominican order. As a Dominican, he was not cut off from the world in a monastery, as are the members of some orders. Instead, he was dedicated to working in the community, in particular by opposing heresy and spreading religious learning and observance. He quickly rose through the ranks, and at age thirty-two became the prior of the monastery of Santa Cruz in the city of Segovia, a position he held for decades.

Favored by Isabella and Ferdinand, he became the queen's personal confessor. He was also appointed to establish one of the early tribunals and by 1483 was overseeing tribunals in the provinces of Castile, León, Aragon, Catalonia, Valencia, and Majorca. In 1488 the king and queen made the ambitious monk the first *inquisidor general* (inquisitor-general or grand inquisitor). This made him the only nonroyal administrator with authority across all of Spain. Torquemada was the natural choice for this position. He was shrewd, a strong leader, and without a trace of scandal in his life. Erna Paris writes, "No surprise, Tomás de Torquemada was [the monarchs'] preferred candidate for Inquisitor-General. He was their close confidant, and even more importantly, no one was ever likely to uncover a hint of human weakness to discredit him or bring the position into disrepute."[57]

In his new position Torquemada had little direct contact with accused heretics; his daily work was primarily administrative, overseeing his vast organization. But his approval was needed for any major decisions or actions, such as setting prison terms, ordering excommunication, or handling legal appeals to verdicts. Torquemada also set forth standardized regulations outlining how regional tribunals should act. And he aggressively expanded the Inquisition into new territory, including Spanish colonies overseas. All of this work was tedious and time-consuming, since several copies of every document had to be written out by hand, and any communication had to be made by horseback messengers across rugged terrain. But Torquemada had a small army of priests and other officials to carry out this aspect of his work.

> **WORDS IN CONTEXT**
> **prior**
> A senior monk in a monastery.

Fear and Admiration

Torquemada inspired both admiration and fear all across Spain. However, the inquisitor-general preferred to stay out of the public eye and lead a quiet, austere life of prayer and devotion to his work—that is, a life that was simple and without luxuries. He was known to wear a shirt of uncomfortably rough cloth under his black robes, to emphasize the need for humility and the willingness to suffer for one's faith. He also

In Their Own Words

The Zeal for Religious Truth

Although Torquemada wrote many documents regulating the Inquisition, other clergymen also contributed their thoughts. One such man was Bernard Gui, a Dominican monk. He wrote what he described as a "short and useful instruction" on what an Inquisitor should be:

> He, the Inquisitor, ought to be diligent and fervent in his zeal for religious truth, the salvation of souls, and the extirpation [extinction] of heresy. . . . He ought to remain calm, and never give way to anger or indignation. He ought to be fearless, facing danger up till death; but while not flinching in the presence of peril, he ought not to hasten it by unreflecting boldness. He must be insensible to the prayers and advances of those who endeavor to persuade him; nevertheless he must not harden his heart to the point of refusing delays or relaxations of punishment, according to circumstances and places. . . .
>
> In doubtful matters he must be circumspect, and not give easy credence to what seems only likely and often is not true, for often that which seems unlikely ends by being true. He must listen, discuss, and examine with all zeal, in order patiently to attain to the light. Let that love of truth and mercy, which ought always to dwell in the heart of a judge, shine on his countenance, so that his decisions may never seem to be dictated by envy or by cruelty.

Quoted in Catholic Apologetics, "The Inquisition." www.catholicapologetics.info.

refused to live lavishly, unlike some clergymen who ate fine food and wore luxurious garments. This self-denial reflected a notably cold personality, as Paris notes: "One can infer something of Torquemada's narrow emotional horizons from his cruel treatment of his only sister, who was entirely dependent on him. Because he chose a rigid, ascetic life she, too, was penniless. Unable to marry without a dowry, she was forced to enter a nunnery in order to eat and be clothed."[58]

Despite his reputation for coldness and austerity, Torquemada may have materially benefited from his position. There is evidence that Torquemada became wealthy, perhaps by acquiring some of the possessions of suspects interrogated by the Inquisition. It is known, for example, that beginning in 1480 he was able to finance the construction of the magnificent Monastery of Saint Thomas in the city of Ávila.

And Torquemada did accept one gift from Ferdinand and Isabella. They provided the funding for bodyguards to accompany him when he traveled—at least forty men on horseback and two hundred on foot at a given time. The inquisitor was rightly fearful of assassination, as Murphy notes: "Torquemada knew that many of his countrymen shared a dim view of him."[59] The powerful monk continued to act as the Inquisition's top administrator until finally retiring at age seventy-two—a very old age by the standards of the time—and relocating to his monastery in Ávila, where he died in 1498.

The High Council

Next to the inquisitor-general, the most important positions in the hierarchy were in the *Suprema*, or high council. This council was composed of five or more senior church officials, usually bishops or archbishops appointed by the pope (but only with Torquemada's approval). Seville, the site of the first Inquisition, became the *Suprema's* headquarters, which occupied the city's cavernous Castillo (castle) San Jorge.

The *Suprema's* main role was to consider difficult cases that regional tribunals were unable to complete. Perhaps there was an especially fine point of church law that had to be carefully considered. Or perhaps the accused person was appealing a decision—that is, challenging it in court.

In such cases the regional court in question sent written reports to the *Suprema*, which discussed the case, examined evidence, and came to a final decision.

To consider these cases, the learned members of the *Suprema* met twice daily. A book of regulations dating from 1674 notes, "All the officials of each inquisition shall meet in the hearing room. They shall work six hours—three before eating, and three after—in summer as well as winter."[60] Typically, morning sessions were devoted to examining issues such as whether a suspect's minor disagreement with church teachings was enough to warrant a trial. The *Suprema*'s afternoon sessions were spent considering cases of minor heresies such as unacceptable sexual behavior.

The *Suprema* had other responsibilities as well. These included giving advice to the inquisitor-general and guiding the operation of the next lower level of administration: regional tribunals. The *Suprema*'s duties in this regard included controlling the finances of the regional courts, resolving debates between regional inquisitors, and clarifying for them the directives of the inquisitor-general. These responsibilities made the *Suprema* the third-most powerful council in the kingdom, surpassed only by the councils of the dominant regions of Castile and Aragon.

Regional Tribunals

The next level down was that of regional tribunals. By 1574 the Inquisition was operating twenty permanent regional tribunals, including five overseas in Spanish colonies. Their primary responsibility was to hear cases in their respective jurisdictions and pass judgment on them. Sometimes these tribunals felt that a case was so difficult or complex that it required the intervention of the *Suprema*. More commonly, however, the regional court had sole authority.

At the head of a regional tribunal were monks or other church authorities—typically two per tribunal—who acted as judges. Torquemada had very specific requirements and standards for any candidate to fill one of these positions. A contributor to *The Catholic Encyclopedia* notes, "The judges were to be at least forty years old, of unimpeachable reputation, distinguished for virtue and wisdom, masters of theology, or doc-

Looking Back

An Efficient Choice of Language

During the period of the Inquisition, an estimated 75 percent of Spaniards spoke little or no Castilian, the standard dialect of Spanish. Instead, they spoke the languages of their native regions. For example, people in the region of the city of Valencia spoke Valencian, their own variant of Spanish. It would clearly be impossible for judges to understand all of these regional languages, so they used Castilian during investigations and trials, relying on translators and interpreters to understand the proceedings. They thus did not force witnesses and suspects to use a standardized language. Historian Joseph Pérez notes:

> From 1560 on, however, the *Suprema* recommended the use of Castilian not for ideological reasons, but simply in the interests of efficiency. [Inquisitor] Soto Salazar, who in 1568 made an inspection of the courts of Catalonia, explained his position in this matter very clearly: "When documents are written in several languages—Latin, Catalan, and Castilian—it is hard to find one's way around them.". . .
>
> Efficiency and common sense dictated that Catalan be used [and then translated]. We are bound to conclude that the Inquisition was certainly an instrument in the service of political power, but it was not used to promote the linguistic unification of the realm.

Joseph Pérez, *The Spanish Inquisition*. London: Profile, 2004, p. 221.

tors or licentiates of canon [religious] law, and they must follow the usual ecclesiastical [church-related] rules and regulations."[61]

The records of a session from Castile in 1483 provide a glimpse into the start of a typical day's work for a regional tribunal. The trial concerned a man accused of several heretical acts. The record states that on the morning in question the judges were seated, with witnesses and secretaries present. A prosecutor stated his intent to try the suspect, who was then brought from the Inquisition's jail by a constable. The record continues:

> The chief prosecutor then submitted a writ of accusation against him. . . . The deputies received an oath from each witness in isolation from the others, as stipulated by the law. In the oath, the witnesses said they swore by God, Holy Mary, and the Words of the Holy Gospels (on which they placed their hands) and by the sign of the Cross (which each of them touched with their right hands), that they would speak the truth about everything they knew and everything they were asked. . . .
>
> The deputies told the witnesses that if they swore and spoke the truth, God might help their bodies in this world and their souls in the next; but if they said and swore anything falsely, God might demand evil for their bodies in this world and for their souls in the next, where they had to stay even longer. The witnesses . . . said they so swore. Amen.[62]

Administration

In addition to directly acting as judges, the two judges heading a regional tribunal also oversaw the large number of bureaucrats below them. Among these functionaries were notaries who attended trials and interrogations, meticulously writing out by hand all necessary records, notes, and other forms of documentation. The huge volume of notes and records that were required meant that these secretaries were kept extremely busy, scurrying from their monasteries or other homes to the Inquisition's chambers and back.

The documentation they created was primarily the minutes of meet-

Prior to the imprisonment or burning of heretics, the court of the Inquisition held a formal trial to determine guilt or innocence even though defendants were almost always found guilty. This oil on canvas painting of the inquisitorial court in session is by Spain's famed classic artist Goya.

ings or forms detailing punishment. Even a light punishment required considerable effort and paperwork. An example of documentation for a minor punishment concerned a silk weaver in the city of Toledo, Alonso Carraza. Carraza was found guilty of uttering a minor dissent to church law and was condemned to public humiliation by standing hatless in church with a yellow candle, indicating shame, during Mass. All of the trial testimony and presentation of evidence was recorded. The judges' verdict also had to be carefully noted. And after Carraza fulfilled his punishment by standing in church with a yellow candle but no hat, proof that this had occurred was needed, so a certificate bearing the signature of witnesses was created and filed. Similarly, when a tribunal seized a suspect's property, each item, even the smallest kitchen utensils, had to be carefully documented. As items were sold to pay for the suspect's upkeep in jail, this information was likewise noted. If the suspect was acquitted, the records helped him or her retrieve belongings that had not yet been sold.

In a 1674 book of rules for trial procedures, regulations were laid out concerning how records were to be kept by regional inquisitors. This book stipulated, for instance, that each tribunal had to keep its records safely stored in a chest or small room. This storage space was to have three locks and three keys to ensure that no one could tamper with the records. The document continues:

> Two of these keys shall be held by the two notaries, and the third by the prosecutor, so that no one can remove any writing without everyone being present. If a notary does something he shouldn't in his office, he shall be condemned for perjury and as a falsifier, and deprived of his office forever; if he is convicted, he may be given a greater penalty of money or exile, according to what the inquisitor-general thinks appropriate.[63]

Comisarios and Familiares

Other levels of the inquisitional bureaucracy were those of *comisarios* and *familiares*. *Comisarios* were village priests who were familiar with their regions and could assist in gathering information. *Familiares*, who were drawn from the lay population, also reported on suspected heretics. *Familiares* were easily identified by the local populace, since they dressed in intimidating black uniforms with the white cross of Saint Dominic on their cloaks. They were sanctioned to bear arms and receive benefits and other privileges. The Inquisition recruited many *familiares*; at one point, the city of Valencia had one for every forty-two residents. A job with the Inquisition, such as being a *familiar*, was a gateway to personal gain such as prestige, extra salary, or pensions. Furthermore, jobs with the Inquisition were often passed from father to son, so families could benefit for generations.

The primary responsibility of *comisarios* and *familiares* was to venture around their city or town, or into the countryside, taking and document-ing denunciations. These were then forwarded to the tribunal's judges. Many rules regulated their actions. For instance, they were required to hear testimony only in the presence of a notary, in order to make sure that testimony was not invented or distorted.

Judges had to be careful when choosing *familiares, comisarios,* and other functionaries from the lay population, in part because they had relatively little education. This is illustrated by a letter that the bishop of Pamplona sent in 1553 to another clergyman. He complained that the *comisarios* in his area were nothing more than uneducated fools, which put their work into question.

In an attempt to raise the quality of the pool of *comisarios* and *familiares,* over the years the *Suprema* issued a series of guidelines. For example, a set of guidelines issued in 1604 stated, in part, "Considering the gravity of the business that must be handled . . . we charge you, sirs, that in the selection of the said *comisarios* you choose well informed, virtuous and discreet persons, and they should have benefices [endowments] or income so that they may be treated with the decency that such an important position requires."[64]

WORDS IN CONTEXT

limpieza de sangre

"Purity of blood," the Inquisition's ideal of Old Christians with no Jewish or Muslim ancestry.

A related problem in choosing lay employees such as *familiares* was that it was usually necessary to confirm their *limpieza de sangre,* or "purity of blood." This referred to the idea that true Spaniards had no trace of Jewish or Muslim heritage in their families. The qualifications needed to prove *limpieza de sangre* varied from period to period and from region to region. For example, sometimes an applicant had to provide legally drawn up family trees or other evidence. Obtaining such information was a tedious process for most job applicants. But such proof was not always necessary. Vose notes, "*Limpieza* continued to be a serious matter for some inquisition personnel . . . but it was always controversial and enforcement was erratic."[65]

The Abuse of Privilege

Those in the inquisitional bureaucracy sometimes abused the privileges of their offices. One example of this concerned an inquisitor, Licenciado

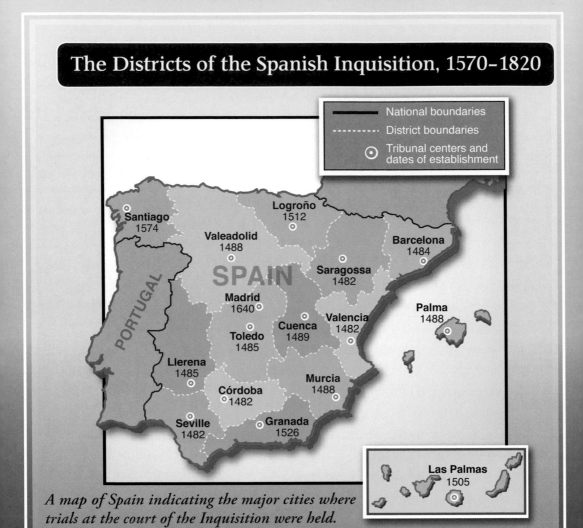

The Districts of the Spanish Inquisition, 1570–1820

Legend:
- ———— National boundaries
- ----------- District boundaries
- ⊙ Tribunal centers and dates of establishment

PORTUGAL

SPAIN

Santiago 1574

Logroño 1512

Valeadolid 1488

Barcelona 1484

Saragossa 1482

Madrid 1640

Palma 1488

Cuenca 1489

Valencia 1482

Toledo 1485

Llerena 1485

Murcia 1488

Córdoba 1482

Seville 1482

Granada 1526

Las Palmas 1505

A map of Spain indicating the major cities where trials at the court of the Inquisition were held.

Gaitan, in the town of Medinaceli. In 1612 the regional tribunal received numerous complaints of Gaitan's cruelty and corruption. These accusations included whipping his servants, stealing money from the church to give to his mistress, and lying in order to ruin the reputation of prominent citizens and others he considered his enemies.

Such abuse of power frequently trickled down to those lower in the inquisitional bureaucracy as well. There were numerous reports, for example, that officials connected with the Inquisition accepted bribes in exchange for reducing punishment or avoiding investigation entirely.

Officials also abused their positions in a variety of petty ways, such as insisting that they deserved to be treated better than other people. In one instance, it was reported that a man in Cordova bought a fish at a seafood market, but refused to give it up when someone else—an acquaintance of a servant of an inquisitor—demanded it. The man was later tried for insubordination and punished with a public flogging.

On another occasion, it was reported that the son of a gardener in Seville—a toddler of two or three—was sitting beside an ornamental pool in the garden of an abbey where the inquisition operated a tribunal. An inquisitor's assistant cruelly snatched a reed that the boy had been playing with. When the boy burst into tears, the gardener angrily asked the assistant why he would do such a thing. An argument ensued, and the gardener was arrested and imprisoned for nine months. Such stories were likely exaggerated, but they indicate an all-too-common abuse of power.

> **WORDS IN CONTEXT**
> **flogging**
> Public whipping of wrongdoers.

Corrupt or not, the Inquisition was able to do its work thanks to a huge bureaucracy of people. They ranged from the highest authorities, the inquisitor-general and the *Suprema*, down to lower functionaries such as secretaries and jailers. This machine was chillingly good at uncovering suspected heretics, hearing accusations and judging their validity, obtaining confessions (often using terrifying methods), and eventually passing final judgment.

Chapter Five

Trial and Punishment

For a suspect, an inquisitional trial was a terrifying stretch of time that frequently lasted years. The victim endured seemingly endless rounds of interrogation by an imposing panel of judges whose purpose was to force a confession. On occasion the judges approved the use of torture to obtain the desired confession, hauling the victim from a wretched prison cell and dragging him (or her) to a chamber filled with dreadful torture devices. Even after confessing, the victim faced almost certain punishment—and sometimes even death.

Moreover, all of this took place behind closed doors. Victims were frequently arrested and imprisoned without any idea why. Sometimes they were imprisoned in cities far from home. They were not allowed to have contact with anyone outside of the jail, including their families, who often had no idea where their loved ones had been taken—or why.

Denunciation and Testimony

The inquisitional trial typically began with testimony from people who accused, or denounced, the victim of some act of heresy. Officials also sought testimony from neighbors or others who could support the accusation by describing incidents in which they had seen the accused engage in sinful activities. Some of these witnesses came forward on their own; others came in response to queries made by the tribunal's investigators. Denunciations could come from any segment of society, including the local priest. Often such accusations were based solely on gossip. In one case dating from 1596, a priest in the region of Catalonia testified that a woman had told other women that her husband could not satisfy her sexually. Although the priest admitted that he had only overheard other women talking about this—not the victim herself—she was put on trial for immoral thoughts and ultimately convicted.

Gathering such testimony was difficult and could take six months to a year. Inquisitors frequently had to travel long distances to collect information, confronting rugged countryside, hostility from local authorities, and the constant threat of bandits. Furthermore, language barriers—roughly one in four Spaniards spoke only their local language, not Spanish—left room for confused, wrong, or distorted testimony.

In Prison

While awaiting word on their case, the accused could spend weeks, months, or even years in prison. Prison provided little more than misery. Jail cells were dark, dirty, and overcrowded. The Inquisition was so zealous in its pursuit of wrongdoers that it jailed far too many people than cells could reasonably hold. Groups of men and women, desperate to contact their families on the outside and subject to terrible conditions, were thus thrown together in close quarters that led, inevitably, to tension and violent fights over such matters as the distribution of food.

Even if food was divided fairly, there was very little of it—and what was available was usually rotten. There were countless other deprivations as well. For example, although jailers sometimes could be bribed to give prisoners pen and paper, the guards also made sure that there was no contact with the outside world—either through letters or by shouting out of prison windows. (And not all cells even had windows.) Representatives of the Inquisition who periodically visited regional tribunals, making sure that they were following rules, frequently heard complaints from prisoners about such conditions. One such inquisitor noted:

> Florian Rodríguez requested that straw be put in the mattress and that the doctor visit him. He also asked for a pigeon because the cow's meat made him sick, and consequently, he had eaten no meat that day. . . . In the matter of coal [for heating], the quartermaster gives one pound instead of two, and the belt that Florian Rodríguez asked for in the last visit still hasn't been given to him.

Torture was regularly employed on accused heretics in order to obtain a confession of guilt. Rooms filled with various instruments of torture, such as the so-called Wheel of Fortune depicted here, were generally located in the buildings where the trial was taking place.

The straw that Florian Rodríguez asked for in the last visit, which he has not received, shall be purchased; the belt shall be given to him, as stipulated; the doctor shall be called.[66]

Deciding Which Cases to Pursue

Determining whether or not a case was worth pursuing was the responsibility of the *calificadores* ("qualifiers"), who examined statements gathered by investigators. If the information seemed legitimate and worth pursuing, in most cases the accused person was summarily thrown in jail.

Not all cases that were investigated went any further than an initial inquiry. In fact, the *calificadores* rejected many as not worthy of further investigation. Any of several reasons might cause this. For one thing, *calificadores* were experts at spotting false witness—that is, invented accusations made out of spite, jealousy, rivalry, revenge, or simple ignorance.

One example concerned a needle maker living in the city of Tarragona. In 1637 his wife, son, and daughter-in-law denounced him, claiming that he spoke out against the church. But the *calificadores* determined that the charges were malicious and untrue, and the tribunal dismissed the case. Another example comes from 1513. According to the official records, a woman accused the wife of a man named Fernando de Córdoba of being a secret Jew. But when presented with evidence that the accuser had made up her testimony, she retracted her earlier statement. The record stated, "She [said that] everything she said about Fernando de Córdoba's wife was a lie. She attributed it falsely so that that woman would come here with this witness, because she is her capital enemy; Fernando de Córdoba's wife persecuted her and caused trouble many times with her husband and deliberately wrecked her marriage."[67]

> **WORDS IN CONTEXT**
> **perjurer**
> Someone who knowingly lies to a court of law.

Perjurers (people who lied to the court) suffered punishments such as whipping or fines if they were caught. For example, Queen Isabella's secretary noted one case in which "poor and vile men who from enmity or malice gave false testimony against some *conversos* saying that they were [secret Jews]. Knowing the truth, the queen ordered them arrested and tortured."[68]

The *Interrogatorio*

Once the *calificadores* reported to the tribunal that a case had merit, the next phase began. This was a question-and-answer period called an *interrogatorio* (interrogation).

Looking Back

A Royal Advisor Converts

Some of Spain's Jews were still unconverted when the Alhambra Edict was announced and were relentlessly pressured to become *conversos*. Prominent among them was Don Abraham Seneor, an advisor on financial matters to the king and queen. Eventually, even this respected member of the royal court was forced to convert. In this passage from his book *The Age of Torquemada*, historian John Edward Longhurst reflects on this:

> The most hard-pressed Jew of all was Don Abraham Seneor. Most of us, fortunately, can coast through life without having to face up to the horrors of self-revelation. But History played a cruel trick on the royal Jew. Ferdinand and Isabella alternately pleaded and threatened. The Jewish community was silent, waiting and watching. Don Abraham had to decide between hard principle and damnable expediency. He waited to the end, hoping in vain for a way out. Finally, he resigned himself, with death in his soul, to baptism and Christian brotherhood with Torquemada, scourge of his own people.

John Edward Longhurst, *The Age of Torquemada*, Library of Iberian Resources Online, p. 157. http://libro.uca.edu.

When a suspect was brought before the judges, he or she was subjected to multiple rounds of cross-examination. This was designed to elicit a confession, if necessary repeating the same questions over and over in an attempt to trip the suspect up in conflicting testimony. Meanwhile, a secretary hiding in the shadows of the interrogation room kept meticulous notes. Even the tone of voice and mannerisms of suspects and witnesses were recorded.

An *interrogatorio* typically took place in a vast room in the castle or monastery where the judges were based. The chambers were intended to intimidate the accused. Toward this end, judges looked down on the accused from tables located on raised platforms or stages. They dressed in white robes and, to conceal their identity, they hid their faces under black hoods. Whenever possible, the judges used techniques meant to intimidate and humiliate the person being questioned. One manual of advice for judges stated, "Have a huge stack of documents in front of you. And as the person is answering questions, flip through the documents as if you have more information than this person could dream of. And every so often, shake your head as if you can't believe what they're saying."[69]

Judges sought to amplify their power and further intimidate the accused by engaging in a variety of small but effective humiliations. Suspects might be stripped of their clothing during interrogation sessions. Or they might be forced to stay awake for long periods between sessions, leading to disorientation and exhaustion.

Further adding to the overall gloom, the only light in the interrogation chamber came from a few candles. Windows—if there were any—were covered with black drapes to block anyone on the outside from seeing the proceedings. The secrecy of the interrogation sessions was unnerving—which was exactly the point. Historian Miriam Bodian comments about the tribunal, "Secrecy was one of the keys to both its power and the terror that it invoked."[70]

Regulations and Rights

In theory, the accused were supposed to be treated with a degree of respect. This treatment was set out in official regulations that, for example, allowed a suspect to sit and keep his own notes while being questioned. A set of instructions to regional judges, written in 1561, stated:

> The inquisitors shall treat the prisoners kindly . . . giving them
> no reason to become dismayed. The prisoners are usually seated
> on a bench so that they can handle their cases more attentively,

although the prisoners have to be standing at the moment the accusation is placed. . . .

If the defendant asks for paper to write down something pertaining to his defense, they must give him numbered sheets of paper which are rubricated [noted] by the notary. The sheets that he is given will be noted in the trial record; and when he returns them, they will be counted, so that the prisoner does not keep paper. It should be noted likewise how the prisoner returned the paper, and precautions should be taken about his writing utensil.[71]

Regulations also allowed the accused to speak for himself or herself. For example, a weaver accused of being a crypto-Jew in 1484 in the city of Ciudad Real denied the charges and asserted that he came from a long line of Old Christians:

I, Pedro de Villegas, appear before your Lordships and affirm my denial of the prosecutor's accusation. If I ate meat . . . on a day when the Church had forbidden it, it was because of an illness I have, which recurred at that time. I caught this illness in this way: my hand was hurt while I was stretching a cloth over a frame, and the frame ripped the cloth in half; the spring came loose and carried me the length of three or four men from where I'd been standing, and it "broke and wounded me," as the saying goes. As a matter of fact, I am debilitated. . . .

If I rested on some Saturdays, it would have been at a time when my job of cloth making wasn't flourishing; there happened to be a month or two during which I did not work at all. This happened two or three times over the year, or on feast days, or days the Church ordered us to observe, or when I was sick.[72]

But the ability to speak for themselves was among the few rights granted to defendants. Most of the time, regulations were simply ignored. Throughout most proceedings, in fact, suspects were kept at a disadvantage. Anyone could testify against them, but the identities of their accusers were almost never revealed. Suspects were also forbidden to bring in witnesses who could testify to their innocence and good character.

Furthermore, suspects were denied their own defense attorneys. Instead, the court appointed a lawyer called a *fiscal*. This lawyer did not primarily defend a suspect—he only tried to convince his client to admit wrongdoing and so spare himself further agony. On the other hand, some *fiscales* did make an effort to defend a client, if the *fiscal* felt that the defendant was innocent. For example, in 1494 in the city of Ciudad Real, the *fiscal* for a woman named Marina González stated to the judges:

> [She] lived, dressed, and spoke like a good Christian woman after she was reconciled. . . . She never wore [fine clothes] that were forbidden at her reconciliation; and even though she wears . . . some little red skirts made of fine cloth, such was not prohibited by [you]. Your Reverences only decreed that her clothing could not be fine scarlet cloth. Therefore, I say that since the accusation is worthless, may your Lords absolve, free, and release my party, promising to return her goods to her, and ordering her released from this prison.[73]

Torture

During the interrogation process, the suspect was given three chances to freely confess. If she or he continued to deny any wrongdoing, a radical form of coercion could come into play: torture.

Torture was rarely used as punishment. Some historians assert that it was never used that way. They argue that it was instead only used as an effective tool for obtaining confession. Evidence suggests that even this use of torture was relatively rare. In most trials it was unnecessary; the interrogation process usually destroyed any thoughts of fighting the charges. On occasion, for a suspect who managed to hold out for longer than the judges considered acceptable, that suspect was forced to watch the torture of another. This was generally enough to induce a confession.

When torture was deemed necessary, any of several methods could be

WORDS IN CONTEXT
fiscal
A court-appointed lawyer whose purpose was mainly to convince his client to admit wrongdoing and thus avoid further agony.

used—all of them excruciating, producing pain and suffering just to the point of death. A suspect might face the *strappado*, in which the wrists were bound behind the back and attached to a rope from the ceiling. When the rope was raised, the shoulders dislocated. Another technique was the *toca*, in which a victim was tied down, a cloth placed over the face, and water was poured over the person's face. This torture technique realistically simulated drowning. Still another torture device was the notorious *potro*, or rack. Torturers put the victim, who was lying on his back, on a rack. Then his arms and legs were attached to large straps. When these were tightened by turning large wheels at either end, all of his joints dislocated.

No matter the method, the Inquisition strictly regulated the use of torture. For example, sessions could last only for a few minutes at a time. Also, a doctor had to be present to monitor the health of the accused. This was because a confession was valid only if the accused could hear and understand the proceedings, and respond accordingly. In other words, a confession was invalid if the victim was so badly injured by torture that he or she was unable to speak in response to questions. Furthermore, if it appeared that the suspect was close to death, the doctor ordered an end to the session.

The Inquisition's representatives were always present, asking questions and recording everything—even the anguished screams of the victim, which were noted dryly and without emotion. Writer Jonathan Kirsch notes that these eerily calm inquisitional records "faithfully recorded every shout, cry and complaint."[74] One example of this documentation quotes a female defendant as stating, "If I knew what to say, I would say it. Oh, *señor*, I don't know what I have to say—oh, oh, they are killing me—if they would tell me what to say—Oh *señores*! . . . I am strangling, and am sick in my stomach."[75]

Judgment and Punishment

Whether or not torture was used and whether or not a victim confessed, the interrogation phase of the trial eventually ended. At this point the inquisitors passed judgment and settled on a punishment. Up to this

Once found guilty, heretics were usually paraded in a public square wearing tall, dunce-like caps and surrounded by priests, monks, and armed guards.

point the trial had taken place in strict secrecy. Now the verdict and punishment were announced publicly, typically before a large crowd that was alerted to the occasion and gathered in the town's main square.

By this point in the process, victims of the Inquisition essentially had no way out. Those convicted of heresy faced some form of punishment. And even if an innocent person confessed and the evidence was inconclusive, inquisitors might condemn them out of their own sense of self-preservation. The judges did not want to appear weak or indecisive by showing mercy. A representative of the pope who observed the Inquisition in Spain in 1565 commented, "The most ardent defenders of justice here consider it is better for an innocent man to be condemned than for the inquisition to suffer disgrace."[76]

If convicted of a minor offense, a condemned person often faced only relatively light punishment. For example, he or she might be forced to fast one day a week or recite certain prayers for a length of time. Or they might be forced to wear a special garment called a *sanbenito* when out in public. This knee-length shirt was a kind of sack made from rough cloth. It was dyed yellow and decorated with large crosses or drawings of dragons and flames representing hell. Being forced to wear a *sanbenito* in public was, if nothing else, a source of intense shame for the victim and his or her family.

More severe punishments included fines, exile, public flogging, or being forced to make long, arduous pilgrimages to far-off holy places. Sometimes men were sentenced to service as oarsmen on the huge ships that transported royalty. This was such hard work that in many cases it amounted to a death penalty.

Ruined Lives

Even those who were acquitted and released usually spent the rest of their lives in shame and financial ruin. Trials cost enormous sums of money, and suspects were expected to pay for food, clothing, transport, and other expenses during the course of the proceedings. A victim's property was automatically confiscated at the time of arrest and sold off to pay these expenses, but most people ran out of money long before a judgment was given. One set of instructions from 1561 tells judges how to obtain money from suspects:

From the sequestered [seized] goods, the constable shall take monies necessary to bring the prisoner to the prison, and six or eight ducats more for the provisioning of the prisoner; no more shall be taken and spent on the prisoner except what he himself eats, what is spent on the beast or beasts on which he is transported, and his bed and clothing. If no money is found in the sequestration, the least valuable goods will be sold until the necessary amount has been raised.[77]

Furthermore, many families suffered deprivation and misery between the time of arrest and the judgment and punishment phase. They were often penniless if—as was often the case—the prisoner had been the family's breadwinner. Communities sometimes tried to help those in need, but there were frequent reports of entire families, including those from prominent households, starving and begging in the streets. Local religious authorities also sometimes tried to help family members, but other times they ignored the problem. For example, during a trial in the 1550s of a suspected heretic, a friar named Bartolomé de las Casas testified on behalf of the defendant, denouncing the regional archbishop for ignoring the victim's family: "As for Carranza's household, the Archbishop of Seville has allowed it to go astray and to be abandoned—its members don't even have anything to eat—though the Archbishop of Seville was entreated many times to support it, as seems just and reasonable."[78]

Autos-da-Fé

Not surprisingly, the most serious crimes resulted in the most severe punishments. According to popular belief, being burned alive at the stake was the worst of these. However, this terrible fate was in fact not a form of punishment. It was instead a final, drastic form of torture—a last-ditch attempt to force a confession. This intent was reflected in the name of the ritual: auto-da-fé ("act of faith").

The first auto-da-fé, in Seville in 1481, was a relatively simple affair. It began with a series of sermons followed by a final offer to convert. Regardless of the answer, six people were burned alive. But the practice

In Their Own Words

Water Torture

This passage from an official record of a 1494 trial describes the use of *toca*, water torture. The victim was stripped of her clothing and tied to a rack with her arms, head, and legs immobilized. The torturers put a cloth over her face and poured water over it, simulating drowning, but she refused to confess. The record goes on:

His reverence [the inquisitor] ordered her to be given water until the three-pint jar ran out; she never said a word. He said that they should take the cord off her head, and she would speak the truth; the cord was taken off, but she said nothing. They tied her up again and began to give her more water from the jar, which they had refilled. He said that they should raise her head so she would speak the truth; they raised her, and she said nothing. When they put her back down again, she asked that she might be raised up, and for Holy Mary's sake, she would tell everything.

Quoted in Lu Ann Homza, ed., *The Spanish Inquisition, 1478–1614: An Anthology of Sources.* Indianapolis, IN: Hackett, 2006, pp. 45–46.

developed over the years into a highly stylized, all-day public event that became almost a regular feature of life for Spaniards. It was essentially a theatrical performance designed to simulate for the crowd the Day of Judgment, the time when everyone must face the final justice of God.

Even if a convicted person repented, death was still certain at an auto-da-fé. There was never a question of living or dying. Only two things were different if a person repented. First, the priests in charge of the ceremony promised the victim that his or her soul of would go to heaven if a final confession were made; a refusal doomed him or her to an eternity in hell. Also, repenting earned the victim death by strangulation, a somewhat less gruesome and painful end—although officials still ritually burned the victim's body after strangulation.

The Alhambra Edict

The peak years of the period when autos-da-fé and other punishments were meted out encompassed only a few decades after the first tribunal was held in 1480. The Inquisition's intensity began to fade in 1492, when it became less relevant to the church. The reason for this drop in interest was a proclamation issued by Ferdinand and Isabella: the Alhambra Edict. This decree ordered the immediate and final expulsion of all Jews from Spain. Judaism was banned and any Jew who refused to leave or convert would be executed.

The decree caused an immediate panic as Jews scrambled to sell off their possessions and leave in the four months they were given. Estimates of the numbers of refugees vary considerably, from as low as forty thousand to as many as eight hundred thousand. It was a bitter time for the Jews. One who chose to stay as long as possible wrote to another who chose to flee, "Do not grieve over your departure, for you have to drink down your death in one gulp, whereas we have to stay behind among these wicked people, receiving death from them every day."[79]

Those who left did so at ruinous cost. With so little time, the refugees had to sell their possessions at a great loss. This was compounded by an order forbidding them to take more than a small amount of money out of the country. An observer of the period noted, "They went round asking for buyers and found none to buy, some sold a house for an ass [donkey], and a vineyard for a little cloth or linen, since they could not take away gold or silver."[80]

Some Jews left but chose to return and become *conversos*. They were typically welcomed back if they were considered to be sincere Catholics. But most stayed away. A handful journeyed to the Americas, but the majority found new homes elsewhere in Europe. Many went only as far as neighboring Portugal, where they were allowed to live until 1496, when that country passed its own law expelling Jews. Meanwhile, the roughly 250,000 Muslims in Spain were allowed to remain, but within a decade they too were being pressured to convert, and by 1614 Islam also was banned and all remaining Muslims were expelled.

The End of the Spanish Inquisition

In the centuries after the Alhambra Edict, the Inquisition gradually lost its power. There were a number of reasons behind this. Notably, the Inquisition's influence waned as the Age of Reason, a major reform movement in European culture and thinking, began to ascend. The Age of Reason (also called the Enlightenment) started in the late seventeenth century. It emphasized reason, skepticism, and scientific inquiry over the superstition and narrow-minded traditions of earlier centuries. In this atmosphere, people in Spain came to see the Inquisition as an outmoded institution—one based on distorted ideas and carried out in barbaric, unspeakably cruel ways.

Nonetheless, officially the Inquisition continued to survive for a long time. In 1826 the last person found guilty by a tribunal was executed, and the Inquisition was not formally closed until 1834. And so ended one of the most terrible chapters in the history of the church, of Spain, and of the people who lived and died during it.

Source Notes

Introduction: The Grip of the Spanish Inquisition

1. Toby Green, *Inquisition: The Reign of Fear*. New York: St. Martin's, 2007, p. 14.
2. Quoted in Lu Ann Homza, ed., *The Spanish Inquisition, 1478–1614: An Anthology of Sources*. Indianapolis, IN: Hackett, 2006, pp. 1–2.
3. Quoted Homza, *The Spanish Inquisition*, p. 66.

Chapter One: The Inquisition Comes to Spain

4. Quoted in Internet Medieval Sourcebook, "Witchcraft Documents," Fordham University, 1996. www.fordham.edu.
5. Kathryn Harrison, "Joan of Arc: Enduring Power," *New York Times*, January 5, 2012. www.nytimes.com.
6. Quoted in Internet Medieval Sourcebook, "Witchcraft Documents."
7. Quoted in *Catholic Sensibility* (blog), "Aquinas on Torture," April 29, 2006. https://catholicsensibility.wordpress.com.
8. Quoted in Henry Kamen, *The Spanish Inquisition*. London: Weidenfeld and Nicolson, 1965, p. 8.
9. Quoted in Anthony Bruno, "Tomas de Torquemada and the Spanish Inquisition," Crime Library, 2014. www.crimelibrary.com.
10. Kamen, *The Spanish Inquisition*, p. 4.
11. Quoted in Homza, *The Spanish Inquisition*, pp. 1–2.
12. Kamen, *The Spanish Inquisition*, p. 256.
13. Quoted in Homza, *The Spanish Inquisition*, pp. 4–5.
14. Anne W. Carroll, "The Inquisition," South Carolina Association of Christian Schools. www.christianeducation.org.
15. Cullen Murphy, *God's Jury*. Boston: Houghton Mifflin, 2012, p. 81.
16. Quoted in Green, *Inquisition*, p. 46.
17. Quoted in Kamen, *The Spanish Inquisition*, p. 34.
18. Quoted in Homza, *The Spanish Inquisition*, p. 6.

Chapter Two: Old Christians

19. Erna Paris, *The End of Days*. Amherst, NY: Prometheus, 1995, p. 20.
20. James B. Anderson, *Daily Life During the Spanish Inquisition*. Westport, CT: Greenwood, 2002, p. 47.
21. Quoted in Kamen, *The Spanish Inquisition*, pp. 124–25.
22. Anderson, *Daily Life During the Spanish Inquisition*, p. 110.
23. Quoted in Henry Kamen, *Early Modern European Society*. London: Routledge, 2000, p. 211.
24. Anderson, *Daily Life During the Spanish Inquisition*, p. 49.
25. Anderson, *Daily Life During the Spanish Inquisition*, p. 58.
26. Quoted in Kamen, *The Spanish Inquisition*, p. 81.
27. Quoted in Henry Kamen, *The Phoenix and the Flame: Catalonia and the Counter Reformation*. New Haven, CT: Yale University Press, 1993, p. 87.
28. Quoted in Kamen, *The Spanish Inquisition*, p. 5.
29. Henry Kamen, "A Society of Believers and Unbelievers," *New York Times*. www.nytimes.com.
30. Quoted in Kamen, *The Spanish Inquisition*, p. 245.
31. Quoted in Homza, *The Spanish Inquisition*, p. 10.
32. Paris, *The End of Days*, p. 181.
33. Quoted in Mary Halavais, *Like Wheat to the Miller: Community, Convivencia, and the Construction of Morisco Identity in Sixteenth-Century Aragon*. New York: Columbia University Press, 2001. www.gutenberg-e.org.
34. Quoted in Halavais, *Like Wheat to the Miller*.
35. Quoted in Homza, *The Spanish Inquisition*, p. 10.
36. Quoted in Homza, *The Spanish Inquisition*, p. 64.
37. Quoted Homza, *The Spanish Inquisition*, p. 166.
38. Quoted in Beth Randall, "Tomás de Torquemada," Jewish World, 1996. http://jewishwebsight.com.

Chapter Three: To Be a Jew or Muslim in Spain

39. Quoted Homza, *The Spanish Inquisition*, p. 66.
40. John Edward Longhurst, "The Age of Torquemada," Library of Iberian Resources Online. http://libro.uca.edu.
41. Henry Charles Lea, *A History of the Inquisition of Spain*, vol. 1. http://libro.uca.edu.

42. Quoted in Homza, *The Spanish Inquisition*, p. 5.

43. Murphy, *God's Jury*, p. 72.

44. Quoted in Longhurst, "The Age of Torquemada."

45. Quoted in Anderson, *Daily Life During the Spanish Inquisition*, p. 95.

46. Paris, *The End of Days*, p. 206.

47. Quoted in Homza, *The Spanish Inquisition*, pp. 28–29.

48. Quoted Homza, *The Spanish Inquisition*, p. 53.

49. Quoted in Henry Kamen, *Inquisition and Society in Spain in the Sixteenth and Seventeenth Centuries*. Bloomington: Indiana University Press, 1985, p. 34.

50. Quoted in Paris, *The End of Days*, pp. 188–89.

51. Quoted in Kamen, *The Spanish Inquisition*, p. 29.

52. Green, *Inquisition*, p. 186.

Chapter Four: The Inquisitors

53. Robin Vose, "Introduction to Inquisition Policies and Proceedings Documents," Rare Books & Special Collections, Hesburgh Libraries of Notre Dame, 2010. www.library.nd.edu.

54. Vose, "Introduction to Inquisition Policies and Proceedings Documents."

55. *Jewish Encyclopedia*, "Spina (Espina), Alfonso de." www.jewishencyclopedia.com.

56. Quoted in Longhurst, "The Age of Torquemada."

57. Paris, *The End of Days*, p. 171.

58. Paris, *The End of Days*, p. 69.

59. Murphy, *God's Jury*, p. 82.

60. Quoted in Homza, *The Spanish Inquisition*, p. 75.

61. Charles G. Herbermann et al., eds., *The Catholic Encyclopedia*. New York: Encyclopedia Press, 1910, p. 36.

62. Quoted in Homza, *The Spanish Inquisition*, p. 19.

63. Quoted in Homza, *The Spanish Inquisition*, p. 74.

64. Quoted in Sarah T. Nalle, "Inquisitors, Priests, and the People During the Catholic Reformation in Spain," *Sixteenth Century Journal*, Winter 1987. www.academia.edu.

65. Vose, "Introduction to Inquisition Policies and Proceedings Documents."

Chapter Five: Trial and Punishment

66. Quoted in Homza, *The Spanish Inquisition*, p. 236.

67. Quoted in Homza, *The Spanish Inquisition*, p. 58.

68. Quoted in Kamen, *The Spanish Inquisition*, p. 18.

69. Quoted in *Fresh Air*, "The Inquisition: A Model for Modern Interrogators," NPR, January 23, 2012. www.npr.org.

70. Quoted in Joan Neuberger, "Episode 10: The Spanish Inquisition," *15 Minute History* (blog), January 30, 2013. https://blogs.utexas.edu.

71. Quoted in Homza, *The Spanish Inquisition*, pp. 224, 227.

72. Quoted in Homza, *The Spanish Inquisition*, p. 19.

73. Quoted in Homza, *The Spanish Inquisition*, p. 38.

74. Jonathan Kirsch, *The Grand Inquisitor's Manual*. New York: HarperOne, 2008, pp. 103–104.

75. Quoted in Cecil Roth, *The Spanish Inquisition*. London: Robert Hale, 1937, p. 103.

76. Quoted in Murphy, *God's Jury*, p. 65.

77. Quoted in Homza, *The Spanish Inquisition*, pp. 223–24.

78. Quoted in Homza, *The Spanish Inquisition*, p. 210.

79. Quoted in Murphy, *God's Jury*, p. 75.

80. Quoted in Kirsch, *The Grand Inquisitor's Manual*, p. 23.

For Further Research

Books

William Henry Giles Kingston, *The Last Look—a Tale of the Spanish Inquisition*. Minneapolis, MN: Fili-Quarian Classics, 2010.

Juan Antonio Llorente, *The History of the Inquisition of Spain from the Time of Its Establishment to the Reign of Ferdinand VII*. London: RareBooksClub.com, 2013.

Joseph Pérez, *The Spanish Inquisition: A History*. New Haven, CT: Yale University Press, 2006.

QUIK eBooks, *True Crime: The Spanish Inquisition*. Eastbourne, East Sussex (UK): QUIK eBooks, 2011. Kindle edition.

Raphael Sabatini, *Torquemada and the Spanish Inquisition*. Looe, UK: House of Stratus, 2008.

Internet Sources and Websites

Anthony Bruno, "Tomas de Torquemada and the Spanish Inquisition," Crime Library, 2014. www.crimelibrary.com/notorious_murders/mass/torquemada/index.html.

This article is part of the extensive Crime Library site maintained by Turner Broadcasting.

Inquisitio, Rare Books & Special Collections, Hesburgh Libraries of Notre Dame (http://rarebooks.library.nd.edu/digital/inquisition/collections/RBSC-INQ:COLLECTION).

This scholarly site describes and quotes from rare manuscripts and is maintained by the University of Notre Dame.

"Inquisition," *Catholic Encyclopedia* (www.newadvent.org/cathen/08026a .htm).

This encyclopedia, part of a website devoted to Catholic news and scholarship, provides in-depth information on all aspects of its topic.

Howard Sachar, "Inquisition in Spain," *My Jewish Learning*. www.myjew ishlearning.com/history/Ancient_and_Medieval_History/632-1650/ Christendom/Inquisition_I.shtml.

This article, by a professor of modern history at George Washington University, is included in an extensive site devoted to Jewish scholarship.

Western and European Chronology, "The Spanish Inquisition: 1478–1834," May 5, 1997. www.thenagain.info/webchron/westeurope/spanin qui.html.

This overview is part of the Web Chronology Project, a site maintained by history professor David W. Koeller at North Park University in Chicago, Illinois.

Index

Note: Boldface page numbers indicate illustrations.

Picture Credits

Cover: The Inquisition in Spain (w/c on paper), Champlain, Samuel de (1567–1635)/Brown University Library, Providence, Rhode Island, USA/Bridgeman Images

Maury Aaseng: 66

© Bettmann/Corbis: 51

© Stefano Bianchetti/Corbis: 56

© Danny Lehman/Corbis: 28

© Tarker/Corbis: 12

Thinkstock Images: 8, 9, 24

Joan of Arc at the stake, May 30, 1431, painting by Frederic Legrip (1817–1871), 1861./De Agostini Picture Library/G. Dagli Orti/Bridgeman Images: 16

Figure of Monk, detail from Miracle of Poison, fresco by Second Master, 15th century, Transept of Upper Church of Sacro Speco Monastery, Subiaco, Italy, 15th century/De Agostini Picture Library/G. Nimatallah/Bridgeman Images: 33

Accompanying the Prisoners Condemned by the Inquisition Court to be Burnt at the Stake, 1610, Anonymous/Index, Barcelona, Spain/Bridgeman Images: 37

The Tax Collector (oil on panel), Roejmerswaelen, Marinus van (c.1493–1567)/Musee des Beaux-Arts, Valenciennes, France/Giraudon/Bridgeman Images: 42

A Muslim school (colour litho), English School, (20th century)/Private Collection/© Look and Learn/Elgar Collection/Bridgeman Images: 46

Court of the Inquisition (oil on canvas), Goya y Lucientes, Francisco Jose de (1746–1828)/Real Academia de Bellas Artes de San Fernando, Madrid, Spain/Bridgeman Images: 63

Inquisition. Instrument of torture. Wheel of Fortune./Photo © Tarker/Bridgeman Images: 70

Entourage Accompanying Two Prisoners with a Priest, Having Been Judged by the Court of the Inquisition, 1860 (colour litho), Spanish School, (19th century)/Private Collection/Index/Bridgeman Images: 77

About the Author

Adam Woog has written many books for adults, young adults, and children; writes a column for the *Seattle Times*; and teaches in a preschool. Woog lives with his wife in Seattle, Washington. They have an adult daughter.